# PUDD[INGS] IN A [PANIC]

## & OTHERS

*Puddings in a Panic* takes the panic out of puddings. Cooking should be fun and what can be more fun than a pudding? Puddings let you play with some great ingredients, ice cream, tropical fruits and of course chocolate ... Puddings should be over the top – an indulgent grand-finale to a meal, an opportunity for creativity and artistic flair.

For many, puddings can be a panic, but help is at hand. Tom Tuke-Hastings is a rising star in the cooking world and one of the UK's leading Cyber Chefs. His inventiveness, neat short cuts and bravado hit the spot whether you're simply in a hurry, caught on the hop or desperate to impress.

Puddings are the last thing you eat in a meal ... they stick in your mind. And even when our bodies are telling us that we're full, there's always a bit of extra room for a pudding. So prepare for glory. Puddings low in panic and sometimes high in calories make the perfect finish for others to enjoy and for you to create.

# PUDDINGS
# IN A PANIC
## & OTHERS

**TOM TUKE-HASTINGS**

**ILLUSTRATIONS BY
NICKY COONEY**

COLT BOOKS
Cambridge

COLT BOOKS LTD
9 Clarendon Road
Cambridge CB2 2BH
tel 01223 357047    fax 01223 365866

First published by Colt Books 2001
Text copyright © Tom Tuke-Hastings 2001
Illustrations copyright © Nicky Cooney 2001

ISBN 0 905899 42 3

Cover illustration by Nicky Cooney
Design by Judith Robertson

Printed in Great Britain by Biddles Ltd, www.Biddles.co.uk

*To my family and Isabella for all their
help and always being there to back me up,
however crazy the idea. And to the Mac
family for being brave enough to take me
on and mad enough to ask me back.*

# TOM TUKE-HASTINGS

At 24, one of the UK's leading Cyber Chefs, Tom first really caught the creative cooking bug in Ireland, where he developed the skill to cook with what was fresh and readily available, and learnt not to be cautious but to cook with flair and bravado. Not one to be tied down by a restaurant, he works around the world and preferably privately, giving him the opportunity to produce highly creative culinary experiences. With *cookingbynumbers.com* his innovative cookery internet site, he is spreading his "cook with what's fresh and available" ethos around the world, too. When time allows, Tom's other passions are being battered on a rugby pitch, skiing the impossible and giving totally over-the-top parties.

## COOKING BY NUMBERS

Tom founded *cookingbynumbers.com* on a simple philosophy. He believes that cooking should be fun and easy. He likes to make the impromptu meal, using what is around in the kitchen, to avoid going out shopping. So he set up a database, which allows people to cook with ingredients they already have in their kitchens, and *www.cookingbynumbers.com* was born. Here you can input the ingredients you have, and it will tell you what to cook and how to cook it. The '*how to cook it*' area is an important element. Without the required skills, you cannot cook the meal. In *skills by numbers* you are taken through the basic skills step by step, accompanied by pictures and video clips. These are also linked, so that whenever they are needed in a recipe, you can click on the link and it will take you directly to the relevant skill. The site has grown and developed, with new ideas and areas being added all the time.

# CONTENTS

INTRODUCTION

# INTRODUCTION

Since Adam and Eve found themselves in the Garden of Eden, mankind has fallen for the temptation of forbidden fruit. From that moment on, the sweet seductive qualities of fruits, desserts and puddings leave a feeling of wicked self-indulgence. After the experience of a delicious meal, crammed with meats, fish, cheeses, vegetables, you still have a need for something sweet. Who cares if you are bursting at the seams already? Puddings, sweets, desserts, call them what you will, nothing else hits the spot, so you may as well give in to temptation.

It is this forbidden fruit aspect which makes puddings so irresistible. This may be why we have them at the end of the meal. Our bodies may tell us that we have had enough, but there is always a bit of extra room for a pudding. If you offer a raw carrot, you are more than likely to be turned down. But turn up with something sweet, sticky and possibly a hint of chocolate in it, and it is amazing how people will succumb. The eating of puddings is a firework display of delights. Chocolate assaults several senses, the silky texture is sensational, the smell is subtle but engulfing, the sight of a yawning chocolate mousse excites the brain, and the taste, when you finally surrender to it, is quite magical. Fruits are bursting with juice waiting to flow when sliced in half; from the tangy lemon to the sweetest wild strawberry there is a host of different flavours and textures. They also give a rainbow of colours to allow you to create a real work of art and beauty. As for the enveloping, lingering qualities of cream, where would the pudding be without it? Strawberries, without cream? It doesn't bear thinking of. Pastry, thin and crisp, a delight to the eye and light on the palette, is itself a blank canvas waiting for you to work your magic.

The possibilities with a pudding are endless: you can refresh, flood, excite and tantalise the tastebuds with an enormous array of flavours. From the sharp to the sensual there is a myriad of different flavours for you to enjoy. Puddings should be over the top. They are an indulgent grand-finale to a meal, making a bold statement about you and your food. There are those who say that they are fattening and bad for you. To that I reply that you do not have to eat a huge amount. Several different puddings a day is not a balanced diet. But then excess of anything is bad.

Some people are allergic to nuts, others may prefer not to serve or eat puddings with raw egg, so these have been flagged where they are included in the recipes.

The aim of this book is to give confidence to the pudding lover. If I can do it, so can you. Relax and enjoy your puddings. They are not as hard as people make them seem. So flick through the book and see what tickles your fancy – then give it a go! Good luck and happy cooking.

# COOKING BY NUMBERS
# MEASURING GLASS

I have had a lot of feedback from the *cookingbynumbers* website about weights and measures. Whilst there are conversion charts on the site, people have their preferences about what units they liked to measure in. To simplify this, I have introduced the *cookingbynumbers* (CBN) measure. This is a pint glass with a scale of one to ten on the side. It also comes with a leaflet showing how to use it and convert weights and measures with it. It can be used to measure weights of dry goods as well as liquid measurements. To simplify the whole process, I have converted all my recipes, including those in this book, into *cookingbynumbers* (CBN) units. This allows you simply to fill the glass to the correct line, with the ingredient in question, and use it in the recipe. This is a quick, international and easy way to get the right amount of produce needed for the recipe. I have included the units throughout the book where appropriate and hope you will find them easy to use. There are, of course, metric units for those who do not have the glass. But I hope that those with one will find it useful for all their cooking and cocktail requirements.

You can order one, £4.99 plus £1.50 for p&p, either online from *www.cookingbynumbers.com*, or by mail order from CBN Measuring Glass, Perrotts Brook House, Perrotts Brook, Cirencester, Glos, GL7 7BS. Please make cheques payable to: *Cooking By Numbers*.

# PUDDINGS
# IN A PANIC

# RAPID RECIPES

These recipes are, as the title implies, aimed at speed. They can be whipped out when the dog eats your lovingly slaved-over creation just before the guests arrive, or when you have a sudden need for a pudding, whether it be personal desire or the unexpected appearance of guests. These recipes are great for the lethargic and time-poor, but just as good for everyone else. So break the emergency glass and let's get cooking.

# APRICOT ZAP

### SERVES 4

This is a great pudding for an emergency and it uses canned apricots, which can hide at the back of the cupboard for ages just waiting for this moment. So whip them out and let them see the daylight. You can, of course, use fresh apricots if you have them, just add enough sugar to make them into a sweet coulis.

> **411g tin of apricots in juice, drained**
> **1 tablespoon Cointreau**
> **175ml** (CBN 2½) **double cream**
> **1 tablespoon caster sugar**

**1** Place the apricots in a liquidiser. Add the liqueur then liquidise until it is a smooth coulis.

**2** Lightly whip the cream with the sugar until it forms soft peaks.

**3** Layer the apricot coulis and whipped cream in 4 wine glasses. Stir gently with a skewer to create an attractive swirl, and serve.

# ANGELS' THROATS

MAKES 20-40

These are a traditional Portuguese delicacy. They are sublime little soufflés covered with a vanilla syrup, which forms a sweet, sticky pile.

**230g** (CBN 7½) **caster sugar**
**½ vanilla pod**
**4 egg yolks**
**I egg white**

**1** Preheat the oven to 220°C/425°F/Gas Mark 7.

**2** To make the syrup, dissolve the sugar in 140ml of water, slice the vanilla pod in two lengthways and scrape the seeds in. Once the sugar has dissolved, bring the mixture to the boil and simmer until it reaches the thread stage (see Note). Then allow to cool.

**3** Whisk the yolks until they are frothy. Then whisk the egg white separately until it is stiff. Fold into the yolks.

**4** Butter a couple of bun tins and sprinkle with flour. Put a tablespoon of the egg mixture in each of the holes. Put in the oven for 5 minutes until they are just set.

**5** Remove from the trays and cool on wire racks. Repeat step 4 until all the mixture has been used.

**6** Using two forks, take the cooled soufflés from the rack, dip them in the syrup and put on a serving plate. Arrange all of them on one serving plate, using up all the syrup and pouring over any that is left over. This is now ready to be attacked by all and sundry.

*Note: The 'thread stage' is reached when the syrup runs off a metal spoon in brittle threads. The temperature should be 102°C/ 215°F, if you want to test it with a sugar thermometer.*

# APPLE SOUFFLÉ OMELETTE

SERVES 2

This is a wonderful way to finish an impromptu romantic meal for two, since it looks impressive but is quick and easy to make.

**40g butter**
**1 tablespoon caster sugar**
**1 dessert apple, peeled, cored and sliced thinly**
**100ml** (CBN 3) **double cream**
**4 eggs**
**2 tablespoons soft brown sugar**

**1** Melt 15g of the butter in a saucepan over a medium heat. Add the caster sugar and mix in.

**2** Add the apple slices to the pan and cook for a few minutes until soft. Turn the heat right down and pour in half of the cream.

**3** Separate the eggs and beat the yolks with the remaining cream and the brown sugar. Beat the egg whites until they form stiff peaks, then fold them into the mixture.

**4** Preheat your grill to medium.

**5** Melt the rest of the butter in a frying pan over a medium heat. Pour in the soufflé mix and cook until the bottom browns. Place it under the grill for a minute or so, until the top browns.

**6** Slide it onto a hot plate, place the apple mix on one half of the soufflé omelette and fold over. Serve warm.

# MARLBOROUGH MESS

### SERVES 6

This is inspired by Eton mess, but I am a Marlborough man and have a love of raspberries. So I couldn't resist adding them. I have used borage flowers. I grow these myself as they are hard to get hold of, even in the summer. If you can't find them, use any sweet, edible flowers.

> **250g strawberries**
> **500g raspberries**
> **80ml** (CBN 2½) **raspberry liqueur**
> **1 tablespoon vanilla sugar** *(see Note)*
> **570ml** (CBN 18) **double cream**
> **10 small meringues**
> **a few borage flowers, to decorate (optional)**

**1** Set aside a few perfect examples of each berry. Chop the strawberries, but leave the raspberries whole. Pour over the liqueur and sprinkle with the sugar.

**2** Whip the cream to soft peaks and fold in the fruit and any juice.

**3** Break up the meringues roughly and fold into the mixture.

**4** Decorate with the perfect berries and a few borage flowers.

**Note:** *To make vanilla sugar, store a fresh vanilla pod in a sealed jar with some caster sugar.*

# STRAWBERRY SABAYON

SERVES 4

This is a marvellous quick pudding. The strawberries are refreshing whilst the custard topping is satisfying and the taste is a delicate mixture of almonds and strawberry.

   100g (CBN 3½) **caster sugar**
   **6 egg yolks**
   **1 teaspoon almond essence**
   **600g strawberries, halved**

**1** To make the custard, place the sugar in a pan with 100 ml of water. Heat until the sugar has completely dissolved and bring to the boil. Remove this from the heat and allow to cool a little.

**2** Preheat the grill to high.

**3** Place the yolks in a bowl and whisk as you slowly trickle the syrup into the bowl. Once it has all combined, place the bowl over some simmering water and stir until it thickens. Once it thickens, remove from the heat and stir until it returns to room temperature. Add the almond essence.

**4** Arrange the strawberry halves in a heatproof dish, so that they fan out in concentric circles. Pour over the custard, place under the grill for a minute to allow the top to brown and serve.

# RUM AND RAISIN BANANAS

### SERVES 6

Most people are used to the rum and raisin combination in ice cream, but it is also delicious with bananas. And you can enjoy this marvellous dessert with some ice cream on the side!

**60g** (CBN 3) **raisins**
**100ml** (CBN 3) **dark rum**
**80g butter**
**100g** (CBN 3) **soft brown sugar**
**6 bananas**
½ **teaspoon cinnamon powder**
½ **teaspoon ground nutmeg**
**ice cream, to serve**

**1** Place the raisins in a bowl and pour over the rum.

**2** Put the butter in a large frying pan over a medium heat. When the butter has melted, add the sugar and stir until it dissolves.

**3** Slice the bananas in half lengthways. Add to the frying pan and fry for a couple of minutes on both sides.

**4** Sprinkle the nutmeg and cinnamon on top. Then pour over the rum and raisins. Ignite the rum and gently stir the raisins until heated through.

**5** Serve two banana halves each, with some of the sauce and the ice cream you have been dying for since the beginning of the recipe.

# PEACH SALAD IN A PINK GRAPEFRUIT JELLY

This is a surprisingly stunning dessert considering how simple it is to make and how few ingredients it needs. Each glass only has a little jelly, so it cools and solidifies quickly.

I teaspoon gelatine
juice of I pink grapefruit
½ tablespoon golden syrup
8 peaches, preferably white, sliced
nutmeg, to grate

**1** Mix the gelatine with a tablespoon of water to allow it to sponge.

**2** Put the grapefruit juice in a bowl and mix in the golden syrup until it dissolves. Melt the gelatine in a bowl over some hot water, strain the juice in and mix well.

**3** Pour into four bowl champagne glasses and place in the fridge to set.

**4** Arrange the peach slices on top of the jelly and sprinkle with a little freshly grated nutmeg. Keep in the fridge until you are ready to serve.

# PASSION FRUIT & RASPBERRY PILLAR

Raspberries and passion fruit are my two favourite fruits and it would be hard to choose between them. So why bother choosing when you can use both and create a pillar of sensual flavours.

>**4 passion fruit**
>**600g** (CBN 18) **Greek yoghurt**
>**4 tablespoons caster sugar**
>**400g raspberries**

**1** Cut the passion fruit in half and scoop out the middle into a bowl. Add the yoghurt and sugar, then beat well until it forms soft peaks.

**2** Reserve 6 perfect raspberries. In a different bowl, reduce the raspberries to a mush with a fork.

**3** In a tall glass such as a champagne flute, layer up the two mixtures. To finish, pipe a swirl of the yoghurt mixture on top with a wide grooved nozzle. Top with a perfect raspberry.

# BANANA COFFEE SHEBANG

SERVES 6

Need to throw something together fast? This is one for you!
The banana coffee richness is beautifully complemented by
the cool, clean crispness of the yoghurt and it is on the table
before you know it.

**6 bananas**
**2 tablespoons instant coffee powder**
**50g** (CBN 2) **soft brown sugar**
**375g** (CBN 11) **Greek yoghurt**
**cocoa powder for dusting**

**1** Take 5 of the bananas, and mush them up with a fork.

**2** Dissolve the coffee in 3 tablespoons of boiling water
and mix into the banana, with the sugar.

**3** Layer the banana mixture with the yoghurt in a glass
bowl, so you have alternating layers of brown and white.

**4** Cut the remaining banana into slices and stick them
into the top. Dust with a little cocoa powder and serve.

# GINGER MANGO
# WITH A BANANA CREAM

### SERVES 4

Don't get stuck with a boring fruit salad: why not go a bit tropical with this mélange of exotic fruit and spice? With the speed of a tornado and a fraction of the mess you will have a pudding fit for the South Seas.

**2 mangos, peeled and sliced** (see Note below)
150ml (CBN 4½) **pineapple juice**
4 tablespoons **crème de banane**
  **or other tropical liqueur**
1 level teaspoon **ground ginger**
275ml (CBN 8½) **double cream**
1 tablespoon **vanilla sugar** (see Note on page 7)

**1** Place the mango slices in a bowl with the pineapple juice, half the liqueur and the ginger.

**2** Put the cream and sugar in a bowl. Beat this to soft peaks and fold in the remaining liqueur.

**3** Divide the mango mixture between 4 bowl champagne glasses, retain a few perfect slices for decoration. Top the mango with the cream, decorate and serve.

*Note*     *To slice mango, first peel the fruit lengthways. Then, starting with the flat side, cut lengthways down to the stone, another cut will remove a long thin slice. Repeat this around the fruit until it is fully sliced and you are left with the stone.*

# ITALIAN LAYERED PUDDING

## SERVES 6

▸ THIS RECIPE CONTAINS RAW EGG ◂

This is a taste of Italy with a few extra flavours thrown in. The panettone and mascarpone mingle exquisitely with the cassis and blueberries to give an exceptional pudding.

**4 egg yolks**
**70g** (CBN 2) **vanilla caster sugar** (see Note page 7)
**500g** (CBN 15) **mascarpone**
**200g panettone, sliced thinly**
**75ml** (CBN 2½) **cassis**
**350g fresh blueberries,**
   **plus a little extra to decorate**
**75g milk chocolate, chopped roughly,**
   **plus a little extra to decorate**

**1** Beat the egg yolks with the sugar until they go fluffy and light. Then beat in the mascarpone well.

**2** Soak the panettone slices in the cassis. Use to line a glass bowl that is about 25cm wide.

**3** Pile about a third of the mascarpone mixture in, smooth it down and sprinkle over one third of the blueberries and chocolate. Repeat this so you have three layers, finishing with a lavish display of blueberries and chocolate.

# A TOUCH OF FLAIR

As I said in the Introduction, expectation is a key feature in panic. These recipes are designed to give you a bit of an edge. They are still quick recipes, but have the advantage of being something a little bit special. May I personally recommend the Passion Fruit Soufflé as a real winner? If you have more time and feel that something even more impressive is expected of you, I hope you have to look no further than the rest of this book.

# CARAMELISED CITRUS CUSTARD POTS

SERVES 6

This is a delicious mélange of various citrus flavours; choose whichever citrus fruits you like best.

**2 oranges**
**3 lemons**
**3 limes**
**I litre** (CBN 30) **milk**
**12 eggs**
**175g** (CBN 6) **caster sugar**
**granulated sugar, to sprinkle**

**1** Preheat the oven to 180°C/350°F/Gas Mark 4.

**2** Grate the zest of each citrus fruit into a separate bowl. Bring the milk to just below the boil.

**3** Separate the eggs and whisk the yolks with the sugar for a few minutes until you have a light yellow mixture. Whilst stirring well, pour the milk over the yolks. Pour this evenly into the 3 bowls of zest. Leave for 10 minutes for the flavours to infuse.

**4** Strain the mixtures separately into 12 ramekins, 4 for each flavour. Then cover each ramekin with foil, and place in a deep baking tray. Fill the baking tray with boiling water to halfway up the ramekins and bake in the oven for about 20 minutes. They are cooked when a knife inserted comes out cleanly.

**5** Leave the pots to cool. To serve, sprinkle the tops with granulated sugar and caramelise under a hot grill or with a blowtorch.

# MACAROON-STUFFED PEACHES

### SERVES 2

This pudding can be made with lots of different soft fruits. Within reason, any fruit that has a hollow in the middle, after it has been cut in half and stoned, should work.

> **3 macaroon biscuits**
> **2 teaspoons sherry**
> **100g** (CBN 3) **ricotta cheese**
> **½ teaspoon ground ginger**
> **2 ripe peaches, halved and stoned**
> **juice of ½ lemon**

**1** Preheat your oven to 180°C/350°F/Gas Mark 4.

**2** Crunch up the biscuits and sprinkle with the sherry. Beat in the cheese and the ginger.

**3** Sprinkle the lemon juice over the peaches.

**4** Divide the filling and pile it onto the peaches. Place on a baking tray and bake for 15 to 20 minutes, or until they are tender and the filling is a golden brown.

# CREAMY CRÊPES CAKE

## SERVES 8

This is not just a tongue teaser, it is also a stunning pudding. It has that wonderful texture of crêpes and creates a delicious, creamy dessert.

225g (CBN 11) **flour, plus extra for dusting**
155g (CBN 5) **caster sugar**
**a pinch of salt**
**4 eggs**
600ml (CBN 19) **milk**
**50g butter, plus extra for greasing**
**2 tablespoons brandy**
**4 egg yolks**
**a little flavourless oil or butter for frying**
**2 teaspoons vanilla essence**
300ml (CBN 9) **double cream**
**225g milk chocolate, grated**
**ice cream, to serve**

**1** Put the flour and 50g of the sugar in a bowl with a good pinch of salt. Beat in the eggs and then whisk in the milk until you have a smooth batter. Melt the butter and add to the mixture with the brandy.

**2** Heat a frying pan over a medium to hot heat. Add a little flavourless oil or butter to the pan and pour in enough batter to cover the pan thinly, rotating the pan as necessary to achieve this. After a short while, the crêpe will free itself from the bottom of the pan. Flip the crêpe and cook for a few seconds on the other side, then place on a plate. Repeat this until all the batter is used and you have a pile of crêpes. Keep the pan hot and add more oil or butter if it is getting dry.

**3** To make a custard sauce, beat the remaining 105g of sugar with the egg yolks and the vanilla essence, until the mixture forms pale ribbons. Then beat in the cream so the mixture is well homogenised.

**4** Take a 20cm cake tin and butter it. Shake a little flour around the tin so that it sticks to the sides and knock out any excess.

**5** Preheat your oven to 170°C/325°F/Gas Mark 3.

**6** Place the grated chocolate in a bowl. Layer up the crêpes with a sprinkling of chocolate and a spoonful of the cream mixture in between each. When you have placed the last crêpe on top, cut out a piece of greaseproof paper to fit on top of it. The paper should stick to the top crêpe, if it does not, lightly butter it.

**7** Bake in the oven for about 30 minutes or until the custard sets. Take out of the oven and leave to rest for 15 minutes. Remove the greaseproof paper and turn out onto a plate, cut into eight slices and serve whilst still warm, with a little ice cream.

# SUMMER FRUIT, TOMATO AND BASIL SOUP

## SERVES 6

This pudding is great fun and a bit unbelievable too. The tomatoes and basil are a bit of a strange idea for a pudding, but it all works really well and tastes great. So if you feel that you are in a rut with puddings, whip this out for a truly ingenious idea.

**300g tomatoes**
**350g strawberries, stalks removed**
**350g raspberries**
**300g redcurrants, stalks removed**
**2 peaches, peeled and stoned**
**juice of I lemon**
**120g** (CBN 4) **caster sugar**
**12 basil leaves**

**1** Plunge the tomatoes in boiling water for a few seconds, then run under cold water and peel. Put all this in a processor: the peeled tomatoes, 200g of the strawberries, 200g of raspberries, 150g of redcurrants, 1 peach, the lemon juice, the sugar and half of the basil leaves. Process to a smooth purée. Put through a sieve to get rid of the pips.

**2** Dice the remaining peach, quarter the remaining strawberries and add to the soup with the rest of the fruit. Serve in a bowl, garnished with the remaining basil leaves – and with a smile as you tell them exactly what they are enjoying.

# PINEAPPLE, PISTACHIO AND VANILLA PARCELS

### SERVES 4

Cooking in foil, greaseproof paper and pastry are well-known ways of keeping in moisture and flavours. The French have been doing it for years and refer to the process as cooking *en papillote*. This pudding retains its grace when served directly from its tin foil coat – just ruffle up the edges and it is ready to serve.

> **200g** (CBN 6½) **caster sugar**
> **100g shelled pistachio nuts**
> **1 fresh vanilla pod**
> **1 pineapple, peeled, sliced and cut into chunks**

**1** Preheat the oven to 180°C/350°F/Gas Mark 4.

**2** Put the sugar in a pan with 570ml of water and the nuts. Cut a slit down the length of the vanilla pod, scrape out the seeds and then cut it into 4 pieces. Add to the pan. Bring this mixture to the boil. Whilst it is heating up, stir well as you want all the sugar to be dissolved before it comes to the boil.

**3** Simmer this for a couple of minutes and remove from the heat. Stir in the pineapple and set aside.

**4** Make four x 20cm squares out of double thickness tin foil. Divide the pineapple mixture between the squares, ensuring each has a piece of vanilla and equal amounts of nuts and syrup. Close up the foil and bake in the oven for 10 minutes.

**5** Remove from the oven and serve in the tin foil packages.

# PASSION FRUIT SOUFFLÉ

SERVES 4

This is without any doubt a brilliant soufflé, and is more than just a wonder to behold. From the second you pull it out of the oven, the smell wafts alluringly at you, tempting you to eat it straight away and forget your guests. If you can resist, they will thank you for producing some of the most sensational, subtle textures and flavours available in a pudding. To top all of this off, it is easy and quick to make. Just don't admit it.

> **a knob of butter**
> **200g** (CBN 7) **caster sugar**
> **6 eggs**
> **10 passion fruit**
> **a little sugar for covering and sprinkling**

**1** Preheat the oven to 180°C/350°F/Gas Mark 4.

**2** Lightly grease 4 ramekins by rubbing a light covering of butter around the inside. Add a little sugar to the first one and swirl the sugar around until the inside is covered. Then shake out the sugar into the next buttered ramekin, tap lightly to remove excess and so on until all the ramekins are prepared.

**2** Separate the eggs. Place the whites in a bowl and 3 of the yolks in another.

**3** Mix the 3 remaining yolks and 100g of the sugar.

**4** Juice 8 of the passion fruit. To do this, cut the fruit in half and scoop all the contents into a sieve with a bowl underneath. Press down with a spoon and move it around until all the juice is in the bowl. You should have about 120ml of juice: use the other 2 passion fruits if necessary. Add to the yolks and sugar mixture, whisking until light and fluffy.

**5** Whisk the egg whites with the remaining 100g of sugar until they form stiff peaks, then fold this into the other bowl of mixture.

**6** Divide the mixture between the ramekins, sprinkle with a little sugar and then place in the oven for 7 to 8 minutes. They are done when they have raised and coloured slightly. Serve immediately with the remaining 2 passion fruits cut in half, so there is one for each serving.

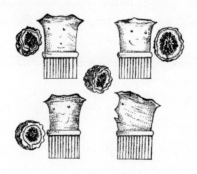

# TRIED-AND-TESTED

If you are in a panic, it can be a great solace to bring out a tried-and-tested old favourite. This takes the pressure off you, as you know it is easy and how to do it. The more you practise a recipe, the easier it becomes and the less you have to consult a cookery book. For that reason, I have included here some of the more old-fashioned recipes. Some have been done before, and they will be done again. But that is their beauty and timelessness.

# BAKED APPLES WITH RAISINS

SERVES 4

I have always had a certain fondness for these since we used to have them at home with apples from the garden. They make a fabulous winter warmer, and work equally well with a cooking apple or a crisp eating one.

**4 cooking or dessert apples**
**100g** (CBN 4) **raisins**
**2 tablespoons golden syrup**
**I teaspoon cinnamon powder**

**1** Preheat your oven to 180°C/350°F/Gas Mark 4.

**2** Using an apple corer or a thin knife, core the apples so you have a round hole all the way through the centre of the apple. Then cut a thin line through the skin around the tummy of the apple. This will allow expansion.

**3** In a baking tray, fill the apples half-way with raisins. Pour a tablespoon of syrup on top of this. Put a pinch of cinnamon in each and top up with the rest of the raisins. Pour the rest of the syrup on top of the raisins and sprinkle on any remaining cinnamon.

**4** Place in the oven for about 30 minutes or until they are cooked. Baste the apples a few times whilst cooking with the syrup which will run out of them. They are cooked when they rise a little and the skin crinkles and browns slightly.

**5** To serve, simply place on a plate and pour any remaining syrup over them.

# CRÊPES WITH ORANGE BUTTER

SERVES 6

These thin pancakes are great on their own, but the orange butter takes them to another level. If you do not have time or the ingredients to make the orange butter, you can, of course, just have sugar and lemon or use a quick filling like chocolate.

**225g** (CBN 11) **plain flour**
**570ml** (CBN 18) **milk**
¾ **tablespoon caster sugar**
**3 eggs**
**3 tablespoons clarified butter** (see Note below)
**4 oranges**
**180g butter, plus extra for cooking**
**200g** (CBN 10) **icing sugar**

**1** Place the flour in a bowl and beat in the milk, sugar, eggs and clarified butter until you have a smooth creamy mixture.

**2** Grate the zest off 2 of the oranges and place in a bowl with the 180g butter. Cream together with the icing sugar, cover and refrigerate.

**3** To prepare for cooking, give your batter a final mix to make sure it is well combined and aerated. Place a small knob of butter in a hot frying pan and move it around until it melts. Pour in enough batter to cover the bottom of the pan thinly. Move it around so it coats the bottom evenly. Let it cook until the bottom has browned lightly and comes loose, flip the pancake and cook on the other side. Once it is cooked, place it on a plate and repeat until all the mix is used. Pile the pancakes on top of each other, separating them with layers of cling film, and place them in the fridge. The recipe makes enough for 2 each and a bit extra in case a couple get stuck on the ceiling.

**4** When you are ready to serve, squeeze the juice from 3 oranges and get the orange butter and pancakes ready to use. Prepare some swirls of zest and cut the remaining orange in slices to garnish.

**5** Melt a knob of the orange butter in the pan and add a pancake. Add a splosh of orange juice and cook until heated through. Fold the pancake onto a plate and garnish with fresh orange slices and a swirl of orange zest. The pancakes can be stored in a heatproof bowl in the oven at 110°C/225°F/Gas Mark ½ until they are all done. Once they are all ready, remove from the oven and garnish individually.

**Note:**  *To clarify butter, heat butter until it melts and separates. Allow this to stand, the golden yellow liquid that settles on top is clarified butter, the white bits should not be used, as they will burn.*

# HOT ORANGE SOUFFLÉS

### SERVES 6

This is a fabulous recipe, which looks especially stunning when the soufflés are served in their own orange shells.

**7 oranges**
**150ml** (CBN 4½) **milk**
**1 vanilla pod**
**4 eggs**
**50g** (CBN 2½) **caster sugar**
**30g** (CBN 1½) **plain flour**
**15g cornflour**
**3 tablespoons Grand Marnier**

**1** Preheat your oven to 190°C/375°F/Gas Mark 5.

**2** To serve the soufflés in oranges, cut the tops off 6 of the oranges. With a teaspoon, remove all of the flesh from inside. This can be used later in a fruit salad or for juicing. Cut a sliver off the bottom of the orange so that it sits straight, but be careful not to make a hole in the bottom

**3** Heat the milk with the vanilla pod in it, bring it nearly to the boil, and then remove from the heat. Separate the eggs and beat the yolks with 30g of the sugar. Once this is combined, beat in the flour and cornflour. Remove the vanilla pod from the milk.

**4** While continuing to whisk the egg, sugar and flour mixture, gently pour in the hot milk. When it is all mixed together this will create a custard. Pour the custard into the saucepan and stir over a low heat until it thickens.

**5** Grate the zest of the remaining orange, and add the zest along with the liqueur to the mixture, then stir until it is well combined. Allow this to cool.

**6** Place the remainder of the sugar with the egg whites and whisk until they form stiff peaks. Fold this into the custard and divide between the orange shells.

**7** Place the oranges in the oven and bake for about 15 minutes or until the mixture rises and browns lightly. Serve immediately.

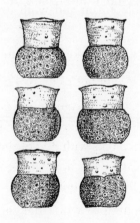

# LEMON SYLLABUB

This is an old favourite that has often come to the rescue. It is one of the quickest recipes I know and one of the simplest. I serve it in separate glasses, which is attractive but also aids the cooling and setting. However, if your ingredients are cool to start with, it should be even quicker.

> **2 lemons**
> **150ml** (CBN 4½) **white wine**
> **75g** (CBN 2½) **caster sugar**
> **275ml** (CBN 8½) **double cream**

**1**  Finely grate the zest of the 2 lemons into a bowl. Add the juice of 1 lemon, the wine and sugar. Mix well.

**2**  Add the double cream and whip until it forms soft peaks.

**3**  Spoon into glasses and refrigerate until needed. Decorate with segments of the remaining lemon and serve.

# VERY
# NAUGHTY
# CHOCOLATE

The very naughty chocolate section reflects my love for all things chocolate. I even feel sometimes that it is a shame to cook with it as cooking and mixing can only subtract from its pure flavour, but this feeling does not tend to last long and I find myself enjoying making increasingly complex and rich chocolate puddings. I love the very texture of chocolate itself, the way it melts at body heat and the endless opportunities it offers both as part of a pudding and for shaping. Whether it be just a single bar, or a mixture of white, dark and milk chocolates to form the centrepiece of a pudding selection, it can either be used in the simplest recipe or expanded into a very complex and time-consuming one. Here are some of my favourite ways of using chocolate.

# CHERRY AND CHOCOLATE TRUFFLES

## MAKES 25

> ⇾ THIS RECIPE CONTAINS RAW EGG AND NUTS ⇽

I adore the taste of glacé cherries – I am not quite sure why, but I think it has something to do with a fondness for Christmas cake. This recipe allows you to use them with a chocolate almond coating to great effect.

**125g dark chocolate, grated finely**
**100g** (CBN 7) **ground almonds**
**1 tablespoon cherry brandy**
**2 tablespoons icing sugar**
**1 egg white**
**25 glacé cherries**
**50g** (CBN 2) **cocoa**

**1** Put the grated chocolate in a bowl with the almonds, cherry brandy and icing sugar. Mix them all together and add enough of the egg white to bind them together.

**2** Leave to rest and firm up in the fridge for 30 minutes.

**3** Divide the mixture into 25 equal parts and flatten out each piece. Enclose a glacé cherry within a piece; work the mixture round to ensure that the cherry is fully enclosed.

**4** Roll each truffle in the cocoa and place in a cool place to set, then arrange and serve.

# CHOCOLATE VESUVIUS

SERVES 6

This is a real explosion of a pudding. A rich chocolate centre oozes across the plate, and contrasts with a solid surround and the dusty lightness of cocoa. This is what chocoholics dream of; an indulgent mixture of hot, sticky, chocolate lava and a firm yet succulent crust.

**250g dark chocolate**
**300ml** (CBN 9½) **milk**
**30ml** (CBN 1) **Cognac**
**50g butter**
**150g** (CBN 5) **caster sugar**
**2 eggs**
**25g** (CBN 1) **self-raising flour**
**25g** (CBN 1) **cocoa powder,**
  **plus extra for decoration**
**whipped cream, to serve**

**1** Preheat your oven to 180°C/350°F/Gas Mark 4.

**2** Break up the chocolate and put it in a pan with the milk. Put over a low heat and stir until the chocolate melts into the milk. Once it is fully combined, add the Cognac and stir it in, then remove from the heat.

**3** Beat the butter with a wooden spoon and cream in the sugar until it takes on a light fluffy appearance.

**4** Separate the eggs and slowly add the yolks to the butter, mixing all the time.

**5** Sieve in the flour and cocoa, mixing as they are added. Then mix in the melted chocolate.

**6** Beat the egg whites to stiff peaks and fold in.

**7** Pour the mixture into a 1½ litre pudding basin. Place in the oven in a bain-marie with 2 to 3cm of water in it. Cook for about 35 minutes or until a crust has formed. Dredge the top generously with cocoa and serve hot with a great big dollop of whipped cream.

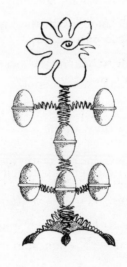

# CHOCOLATE BAVARIAN

SERVES 8

This is a rich chocolate mousse on a tasty cooked biscuit base.

**8 digestive biscuits**
**75g butter**
**25g** (CBN I) **soft brown sugar**
**I x chocolate mousse recipe** *(see page 46)*
**icing sugar, to decorate**

**1** Preheat the oven to 180°C/350°F/Gas Mark 4.

**2** Put the digestive biscuits in a bag and break them into crumbs using your hands and a rolling pin.

**3** Melt the butter and mix in the biscuit crumbs and sugar. Push this into a 24cm tart tin so it covers the sides and bottom evenly. Cook in the oven for 6 minutes. Once it is cooked, set aside to cool.

**4** Make the chocolate mousse following the recipe on page 46, fill the tart tin with the mousse and allow to set in the fridge.

**5** Before serving, dust lightly with icing sugar.

# CHOCOLATE YOGHURT BRICK

SERVES 6

This is so named because the result is a wonderful brick-shaped dessert. But fear not, the texture is not like a brick – on the contrary, it simply melts in your mouth. You do not even need to melt the chocolate to make this, so there are no excuses for failing to indulge.

**275ml** (CBN 8) **Greek yoghurt**
**275ml** (CBN 8½) **double cream**
**40g dark chocolate, grated**
**raspberries, or other fruit (optional)**
**75g** (CBN 3) **soft brown sugar**

**1** Place the yoghurt and cream together in a bowl. Add the grated chocolate.

**2** Whip this mixture until it holds a peak, by hand or with a machine. Place in a loaf tin lined with clingfilm, for the signature shape. If you wish, you can cover the bottom of the container with a complementary fruit such as raspberries.

**3** Sprinkle the sugar over it, cover and refrigerate for at least an hour or overnight if you have the time.

# CHOCOLATE MASSACRE

### SERVES 12

This is so called because it makes death by chocolate look like a teddy bears' picnic. Layers of chocolate genoise (sponge cake) are coated with a thick ganache (sticky creamy chocolate goo) and this is all then covered with more chocolate to make a pudding to be scared of.

> **375g dark chocolate, plus extra to decorate**
> **3 tablespoons strong black coffee**
> **5 eggs**
> **125g** (CBN 4) **caster sugar**
> **570ml** (CBN 18) **double cream**
> **200g milk chocolate**
> **200g white chocolate**

**1** Preheat your oven to 180°C/350°F/Gas Mark 4.

**2** Place a heatproof bowl over simmering water and then melt 175g of the dark chocolate with the coffee.

**3** Separate the eggs and beat the yolks until they are smooth and pale. Add the cool but liquid chocolate to this mixture and beat in until it is fully combined.

**4** Whisk the sugar and egg whites until they form stiff glossy peaks. Fold into the chocolate mixture. Place this in a 33cm by 23cm swiss roll tin lined with greaseproof paper and bake in the oven for about 15 minutes. Once it has puffed up, remove it. Set to one side to cool, you have now made the genoise.

**5** Heat the cream in a pan over a medium heat and melt the remaining dark chocolate and the milk chocolate in it.

Once they have melted, cover with clingfilm and place in the fridge to cool. This is the ganache.

**6** To assemble, cut the genoise in three so you have three 11cm by 23cm pieces. Beat the chilled ganache until it forms very stiff peaks. Place a layer of genoise on the serving dish and cover it with ganache; repeat this until you have layered up all the genoise, but make sure enough ganache is left to cover all the sides.

**7** Melt the white chocolate and pour it on greaseproof paper to make rectangles to coat the pudding. When it is nearly set but still soft, cut it into 12 strips 2cm wide; these need to be long enough to go up one side, over the top and down the other. Measure the pudding and cut them into three, so you have two the right size for the sides and one for the top. This will make it easy to serve the pudding. You will also need two bigger pieces that can cover the ends.

**8** Once the chocolate has set, use the white chocolate rectangles to cover it and place the larger tiles on the end. This should leave you with a gleaming white casing of chocolate.

**9** Decorate with dark chocolate curls to contrast and serve.

**Note:** *To make chocolate curls, take a bar of chocolate of any colour, the thicker the better. Heat it a little with the palm of your hand. Once it has softened (but not melted), use a round pastry cutter to scrape off a curl. As it goes along, the chocolate curls. Repeat as needed.*

# AUSSIE CHOCOLATE MINT CHEESECAKE

SERVES 6

I first had this cheesecake at a barbecue in the deep outback of central western Queensland in Australia. I liked it so much I begged for the recipe. I persisted and eventually was entrusted with the family secret of how to make this fabulous pudding.

> 12 digestive biscuits
> 45g butter
> 1 tablespoon of cocoa
> 250g (CBN 7½) cream cheese
> 100g (CBN 3½) caster sugar
> 1 teaspoon vanilla essence
> 1 teaspoon gelatine
> 250ml (CBN 8) cream
> 6 solid chocolate after-dinner mints
> chocolate, for making curls (see Note page 39)

**1** The first thing we need to make is the base. To do this, crush the biscuits. I like to put them in a bag and hit them with a wooden rolling pin until they form crumbs.

**2** Then melt the butter and mix in the cocoa and the biscuit crumbs. Put this mixture in a 24cm loose based tin. Push the mixture right into the edges of the tin and all around the base and up the sides, so that the tin is evenly covered with the compacted biscuit mix. Place in the fridge while you make the filling.

**3** Beat the cream cheese, sugar and vanilla essence together, until smooth and creamy.

**4** Sponge the gelatine in a tablespoon of water and allow it to soak it up. Melt the gelatine, by putting the bowl it is in over hot water. Put a spoonful of the cream cheese mixture into the gelatine and stir it in, then add this to the rest of the cream cheese and mix well.

**5** Beat the cream until it forms soft peaks and fold it into the cream cheese mixture. Pour this into the biscuit base.

**6** Break up the chocolate mints and put in a bowl with a tablespoon of water. Put the bowl over a pan of hot water and stir until melted. Pour the melted chocolate over the filling, then use a skewer to swirl the mixture to create a circular pattern in the chocolate.

**7** Chill for at least 30 minutes until set, remove from the tin, sprinkle with chocolate curls and serve with single cream.

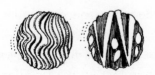

# CHOCOLATE STRAWBERRY PAVLOVA

## SERVES 8

➤ THIS RECIPE CONTAINS RAW EGG ◄

This version is better than your average pavlova since it combines the typical light fruitiness of a pavlova with a dose of exciting chocolate action.

**6 egg whites**

**375g** (CBN 12) **caster sugar**

**butter, to grease**

**icing sugar, to sprinkle**

**200g dark chocolate**

**4 egg yolks**

**300ml** (CBN 9½) **double cream**

**I tablespoon strawberry liqueur**

**200g strawberries, destalked and quartered**

**100g milk chocolate, chopped roughly**

**1** Preheat your oven to 150°C/300°F/Gas Mark 2.

**2** First we need to make the meringues. To do this, whisk the egg whites with 350g of the sugar until they form stiff peaks. Fill a piping bag with the mixture. Lightly butter enough greaseproof paper for the two 22cm circles and sprinkle it lightly with icing sugar. Make two 22cm circles on the greaseproof paper. Then place it in the oven for 30 minutes. Then turn the oven temperature down to 130°C/250°F/Gas Mark ½ and cook for a further hour.

**3** Whilst this is going on, we can start on the filling. Melt the dark chocolate with a few tablespoons of water in a bowl over simmering water. One by one mix the egg yolks into the melted chocolate over the simmering water. Keep mixing them until you have a rich smooth mix that has thickened a little. Then remove from the heat.

**4** Whip the cream with the rest of the sugar and the liqueur until it holds a peak.

**5** When you are ready to assemble the pudding, get all the pieces together. Spread the chocolate on one of the meringue circles. Fold the strawberries into the cream, with the chopped milk chocolate. Spread this on and top the whole thing with the final meringue circle. Serve this within the hour, as the moisture will destroy the meringue.

# DARK AND WHITE CHOCOLATE CHEESECAKE

SERVES 8

This lovely rich cheesecake makes the most of both white and dark chocolate, which work so well together.

200g chocolate biscuits
80g butter
1 tablespoon soft brown sugar
250g dark chocolate
375g cream cheese
125g (CBN 4) caster sugar
3 eggs
150g white chocolate
160g (CBN 5) sour cream

**1** Preheat your oven to 180°C/350°F/Gas Mark 4.

**2** Butter a 24cm round baking tin and then line with greaseproof paper, allowing it to go over the sides. Break up the biscuits by putting them in a clean bag and hitting them gently with a rolling pin until they form crumbs. Melt the butter and the brown sugar together,

then mix this into the biscuit crumbs. Push the biscuit crumbs into the bottom and edges of the tin.

**3** Chop 100g of the dark chocolate into small pieces and sprinkle over the biscuit base.

**4** Beat the cream cheese in a bowl, and when soft beat in the sugar. Beat in the eggs one at a time until they mix in smoothly. Melt the white chocolate in a bowl over just simmering water. When it has melted, mix it into the cream cheese and beat until smooth. Pour this over the base and spread evenly. Put this in the oven for about 30 minutes or until it has set. Once cooked, allow to cool and then refrigerate. Once it has set firm it is ready to have the top layer applied.

**5** Put the remaining dark chocolate in a pan with the sour cream. Mix well over a low heat until the chocolate and the cream combine. Spread this mixture on the top of the cheesecake and allow to set. Cut it into 8 portions and serve.

# DARK CHOCOLATE MOUSSE

SERVES 6

➤ THIS RECIPE CONTAINS RAW EGG ◀

This wonderful pudding is served all over the world. Here is the basic recipe, to which you can add liqueurs, grated rind, marshmallows or whatever you want, to give a myriad of variations.

**25g butter**
**200g dark chocolate**
**4 eggs**

**1** Place the butter and chocolate in a pan with 2 table-spoons of water. Melt over a very low heat and remove from the heat.

**2** Separate the eggs and beat the yolks into the chocolate one by one.

**3** Beat the egg whites to stiff peaks and fold into the cooled chocolate mixture.

**4** Place into a bowl or glasses and chill for at least 30 minutes for glasses and an hour for a bowl.

# FLOATING ISLANDS ON A CHOCOLATE SEA

SERVES 6

These 'poached' meringues are very subtle in texture and are set off superbly by a sea of chocolate custard sauce. It is the sort of pudding which guests always find room for, even after a large and delicious meal.

**6 eggs**
**300g** (CBN 10) **caster sugar**
**570ml** (CBN 18) **milk**
**50g dark chocolate**

**1** Separate the eggs, and whisk the whites with 250g of the sugar. Keep going until they form glossy stiff peaks.

**2** To cook the meringues, heat the milk so it is just below boiling. Take generous tablespoons of the egg white mixture and poach in the milk. Cook in batches so the pan is not too crowded. After a couple of minutes cooking, turn them and cook the other side. They are cooked once they firm up. Allow to drain on a plate.

**3** Sieve the milk and return to the pan.

**4** To make the custard, beat the egg yolks and the rest of the sugar together until light and fluffy. Mix this well into the milk and stir over a low to medium heat until it thickens enough to cover the back of a spoon. Once it thickens, remove from the heat and set to one side.

**5** Melt the chocolate and add to the custard.

**6** To serve, pool some of the chocolate custard on a plate and place the poached meringues on top.

# DOUBLE CHOCOLATE VELVET

### SERVES 10

This is the epitome of smooth, sensual chocolate, which just melts in your mouth and should only be attempted by serious chocoholics.

**520g dark chocolate**
**3 tablespoons strong black coffee**
**7 eggs**
**145g** (CBN 5) **caster sugar**
**55g butter**
**225g milk chocolate**
**35ml** (CBN 1) **kirsch**
**35ml** (CBN 1) **rum**
**330ml** (CBN 10) **double cream**
**a little white chocolate, to decorate (optional)**

**1** Preheat your oven to 180°C/350°F/Gas Mark 4.

**2** Line a 32.5cm by 23cm swiss roll tin with greaseproof paper.

**3** To make the genoise, melt 175g of the dark chocolate in the coffee in a pan over a low heat. Separate the eggs and beat 5 yokes with 125g of the caster sugar until the mixture is light and fluffy. Once the chocolate has melted, remove it from the heat and beat in the yolk and sugar mixture.

**4** Beat 5 whites into stiff peaks and fold them into the chocolate mixture. Pour this into the tin and bake in the oven for 15 minutes. Remove from the oven and allow the genoise to cool in the tin.

**5** Line a 1 litre pudding basin with tin foil. Remove the cooled genoise from the tin and take off the greaseproof paper. Cut a square from the genoise to cover the bottom of the basin and then cut the rest of the genoise into strips and use to cover the sides of the basin.

**6** For the filling, melt the butter with 225g of dark chocolate and all of the milk chocolate. Beat the remaining 2 egg yolks with the spirits and then mix in the molten chocolate.

**7** Whip the cream until it holds a peak and fold in the chocolate mixture. Place the 2 egg whites with the remaining caster sugar and whip to stiff peaks, then fold in the cream and chocolate mixture.

**8** Place this mixture in the pudding basin and, if you have any genoise left, you can put it on the top. Cover and leave to chill in the fridge for at least 2 hours.

**9** To make the icing, melt the remaining 120g of dark chocolate in 2½ tablespoons of boiling water and then beat together. Turn the pudding out of the pudding basin and ice your creation. To decorate, I like to melt white chocolate, and pipe it on top to create a great contrast.

# CHOCOLATE APPLE SOUFFLÉ

SERVES 4

This is a bit of a twist on the old favourite, the chocolate soufflé. The apple adds an excellent new dimension to its wonderful flavours and texture.

2 eating apples, cored, peeled and sliced thinly
15g butter, plus extra for greasing
125ml (CBN 4) strong black coffee
125g dark chocolate
3 egg yolks
½ teaspoon vanilla essence
5 egg whites
30g (CBN 1) caster sugar
vanilla ice cream, to serve

1 Cook the apple slices in the butter over a medium heat until a purée forms.

2 Put the coffee in a pan over a low heat. Add the chocolate and stir until it melts. Remove from the heat and beat in the 3 egg yolks, the apple purée and the vanilla essence.

3 Preheat the oven to 220°C/425°F/Gas Mark 7. Butter 4 ramekins.

4 Whip all 5 egg whites, adding the sugar slowly until they form stiff peaks. Heat the chocolate mixture and stir in one quarter of the egg whites; then fold in the rest.

5 Divide the mixture between the ramekins and bake in the oven for about 12 to 15 minutes. They are ready when they rise and form a crust on the top. Serve immediately with some vanilla ice cream.

# WHITE CHOCOLATE MOUSSE

SERVES 6

➤ THIS RECIPE CONTAINS RAW EGG ◀

White chocolate has a very smooth, rich flavour and this mousse exploits it to the full. It is rich and very satisfying.

**255g finest white chocolate**
**5 egg yolks**
**2 teaspoons gelatine powder**
**450ml** (CBN 14) **double cream**

**1** Melt the white chocolate gently in a bowl over some just-simmering water. Remove from the heat and beat in the egg yolks one by one. Keep going and do not stop – it may look as if it is going grainy and solid as if going into a block – but keep at it until you have a smooth mixture.

**2** Sponge the gelatine in a couple of tablespoons of water. Heat it over simmering water until it dissolves, and then mix it into the chocolate.

**3** Whip the cream to soft peaks and fold in the chocolate. Pour into a bowl or glasses and leave in the fridge for at least 2 hours to set. Garnish and serve.

# FROSTHEAVE CHOCOLATE CAKE

This old family recipe is named after a geographical feature, that is found on glaciers. This cake is great and makes an unusual end to a meal, especially when partnered with fresh fruits and lashings of thick clotted cream.

110g margarine
110g (CBN 4) **soft brown sugar**
110g golden syrup
150ml (CBN 4½) **milk**
1 egg
½ **teaspoon bicarbonate of soda**
175g (CBN 9) **self-raising flour**
2 tablespoons cocoa powder
**To serve:**
seasonal fruit, sliced
clotted cream

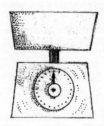

**1** Preheat the oven to 180°C/350°F/Gas Mark 4.

**2** Melt the margarine with the sugar and syrup in a pan over a medium to low heat.

**3** Mix the milk and egg and stir into the mixture until it is all combined.

**4** Combine the remaining ingredients and sift onto the mixture, then fold in.

**5** Line a 20cm cake tin with greaseproof paper. Pour in the mixture and bake in the oven for 30 minutes. The cake is ready when a skewer pushed into the centre comes out clean. The top will have split to look like its namesake.

**6** Arrange with some prepared seasonal fruit and cream, then serve.

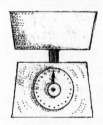

# STEAMED CHOCOLATE PUDDING WITH VANILLA CREAM

## SERVES 6

Steamed puddings can conjure up all sorts of associations; for some it's school dinners and custard that would put the India rubber company to shame. But this chocolate pudding is light, delicious and full of flavour.

> **125g butter, plus extra for greasing**
> **125g** (CBN 4) **caster sugar**
> **2 eggs**
> **2 tablespoons milk**
> **175g** (CBN 9) **flour**
> **1 teaspoon baking powder**
> **25g** (CBN 1) **cocoa powder**
> **2 tablespoons vanilla sugar** *(see Note on page 7)*
> **250ml** (CBN 9) **double cream**

**1** Cream the butter with the caster sugar until it is light and fluffy.

**2** Beat the eggs in one by one and, once the mixture has combined well, add the milk.

**3** In a separate bowl, mix together the flour, baking powder and cocoa. Mix this into the eggs and butter gently.

**4** Rub the inside of a 1 litre pudding basin with a little butter. Pour in the mixture and cut out a circle of grease-proof paper to go directly on top.

**5** Then cover the bowl with another sheet of grease-proof paper with a couple of folds in the middle so it can expand. Tie this down firmly with string.

**6** Place on an upturned saucer in a large saucepan. Add about 10cm of hot water, put the lid on and simmer for about 1½ hours. Keep checking to make sure that it does not boil dry.

**7** Whilst this is going on, mix the vanilla sugar with the cream and whip to soft peaks. Cover and leave in the fridge to allow the flavours to develop until serving.

**8** When the pudding is cooked, remove all of the greaseproof paper, turn it out onto a plate and serve with the vanilla cream.

# FROZEN CHOCOLATE SPONGE

## SERVES 8

▼ THIS RECIPE CONTAINS RAW EGG ◀

Unlike a lot of frozen cakes, this recipe actually contains
cake. The cool chocolate centre is enveloped in chocolate
icing to add a little more indulgence for those who were
even tempted to think that it did not have enough.

> **9 egg yolks**
> **75g** (CBN 2½) **caster sugar**
> **I teaspoon vanilla essence**
> **5 tablespoons flour**
> **a pinch of salt**
> **12 egg whites**
> **500g dark chocolate**
> **50ml** (CBN 1½) **brandy**
> **2 tablespoons black coffee**
> **270ml** (CBN 8½) **double cream**

**1** The first thing you need to do is make the sponge
cake. Set the oven for 190°C/375°F/Gas Mark 5. Beat 7
yolks with the sugar and vanilla essence, until the mixture is creamy and pale.

**2** Fold in the flour with a pinch of salt. Whisk 7 egg
whites until they form firm peaks and fold them in.
Grease two 32.5cm by 23cm swiss roll tins and line them
with greaseproof paper. Divide the mixture between the
two and place them in the oven.

**3** Bake for 15 to 20 minutes or until they are spongy.
Remove from the oven and allow to cool. Once cooled,
empty out and carefully remove the greaseproof paper.

**4** Line a 20cm cake tin with a circle of greaseproof paper. Cut a circle of sponge big enough to fit the bottom and place it in the tin. Cut another circle of sponge the same size and place it to the side. Use the rest of the sponge to line the sides of the tin, cutting and shaping as necessary.

**5** Break up 350g of the chocolate and place it in a pan with the brandy and the coffee. Cook over a low heat, stirring all the time. When the chocolate has melted and formed a paste, remove it and allow it to cool to room temperature.

**6** Once the chocolate has cooled, beat in the two yolks one at a time. Whisk the remaining 5 egg whites until they form stiff peaks and fold in. Whisk 120ml of the cream until it is similarly stiff and fold into the mixture as well. Pour this into the cake tin and top with the circle of cake. Cover with tin foil and freeze for at least 3 hours.

**7** When frozen, remove from the tin and remove the greaseproof paper. Ice it by melting the remaining 150g of chocolate in the 150ml of double cream over a medium heat. Allow this to cool a little and pour over the cake, icing it evenly. Return it to the freezer until you are ready to serve it.

# SURPRISE CHOCOLATE MOUSSE

### SERVES 8

➤ THIS RECIPE CONTAINS RAW EGG ◄

I love surprises and this is a lovely little bit of intrigue. As you break through the dark chocolate mousse, you find a white chocolate centre with a raspberry coulis heart in a chocolate cup.

> **75g milk chocolate, plus extra to decorate**
> **100g raspberries**
> **1 tablespoon caster sugar**
> **1 x white chocolate mousse recipe** *(see page 51)*
> **½ x dark chocolate mousse recipe** *(see page 46)*

**1** First, make the chocolate cup. Melt the chocolate and then coat the inside of a disposable plastic cup halfway up with the melted chocolate. Put it in the fridge to set. Pour the rest of the chocolate onto a sheet of greaseproof paper to make a flat piece of chocolate big enough to cover the top of the cup. Once the chocolate in the cup is thick enough and set, you can cut the cup off it.

**2** To make the raspberry coulis, liquidise the raspberries with the sugar and pass through a sieve to remove all pips.

**3** Now make the white chocolate mousse. Place the chocolate cup in the centre of a large bowl but don't use a glass bowl or it won't be much of a surprise. Fill the chocolate cup with the coulis, and cover the top with the flat piece of chocolate. Pour the white chocolate mousse into the bowl and place in the fridge to set.

**4** Make the dark chocolate mousse and pour on top of everything. Return to the fridge for at least 30 minutes or until set. Decorate the top with chocolate curls. (see Note page 39)

**5** To serve, take a large spoon and dive through the mousses into the coulis in the chocolate cup and give each person a mix of all three.

# WHITE CHOCOLATE SOUFFLÉ

## SERVES 6

This is a wonderful way to display the rich buttery taste of white chocolate. It is hot and fluffy – the perfect end to any meal.

**250g white chocolate**
**50ml** (CBN 1½) **cream**
**2 tablespoons milk**
**6 eggs**
**40g** (CBN 1½) **caster sugar**
**1 teaspoon vanilla essence**
**butter, for greasing**

**1** Preheat your oven to 200°C/400°F/Gas Mark 6.

**2** Melt the chocolate, cream and milk in a bowl over simmering water. Once it has melted, remove from the heat.

**3** Separate the eggs and beat the yolks into the chocolate one by one. Once well mixed in, add the sugar and vanilla essence.

**4** Butter 6 ramekins. Whisk the egg whites until they form stiff peaks. Fold them into the chocolate mix and fill the 6 ramekins. Bake in the oven for about 15 to 20 minutes.

**5** Once they have risen and browned on top, they are ready. Rush them to the table and serve immediately.

# TARTS
# HEAVEN

I have spent many a holiday in France
and eaten far too many of their
delicious pastries. It was therefore
inevitable that, when I started cooking, they became a very important
part of my cookery arsenal. The
whole premise of a tart is wonderful:
there is a pastry case and you cram it
full of the most delicious ingredients
you can lay your hands on. It can be
simple and plain like my old friend
Tarte Tatin or more complex and full
of sensational flavours like the
Rhubarb and Frangipane Tart. Tarts
can of course be made in an array of
different shapes and sizes. I have tried
to keep mainly to one size, to make it
easier to follow and reduce the need
for too much equipment. I hope that
these tarts will turn you into an
enthusiast as well.

# BASIC TART BASE

For most of the tarts in this book, I use the same pastry. The recipe is simple and makes enough for one 24cm tart base. If you are filling it with a cold filling, you might want to brush melted chocolate around the inside to make it extra special.

115g (CBN 6) **plain flour, sifted**
**75g butter**
**1 dessertspoon caster sugar**
**1 egg**
**milk, for the egg wash**

**1** With your fingers, rub the flour and butter together in a bowl, until they resemble breadcrumbs, then add the sugar.

**2** Beat the egg and mix in half of it. Depending on how dry the ingredients are, you may need a little water to bring this all together into a dough. Lightly knead to ensure it is all mixed smoothly. Place in the fridge for 30 minutes so that it can rest.

**3** Preheat the oven to 200°C/400°F/Gas Mark 6.

**4** Roll the pastry on a lightly floured surface so it is about 3mm thick. Line a greased 24cm tart tin, pushing the pastry into all the nooks and crannies. Trim off the top.

**5** To bake blind, prick the base with a fork and cover with greaseproof paper. Weigh this down with dried beans. Bake for 15 minutes; then remove the paper and beans

**6** Brush lightly all over with egg wash made from the rest of the egg mixed with a little splash of milk. Bake for a further 5 to 10 minutes until lightly browned. It is now ready for use.

# TARTE AUX FRAMBOISES

## SERVES 8

At one point this was my signature pudding. The shiny red glaze makes it look very professional and people will be asking how you manage to import fresh tarts from France. For an extra treat, paint the base with melted chocolate before you fill it.

**1 x pastry ingredients** *(see page 63)*
**250g cream cheese, mascarpone is excellent**
**1 tablespoon vanilla sugar** *(see Note on page 7)*
**500g raspberries**
**3 tablespoons redcurrant jelly**
**1 tablespoon Grand Marnier**
**redcurrant leaves, to decorate (optional)**
**melted chocolate (optional)**

**1** Make the pastry to the end of step 5 on page 63, then allow to cool.

**2** To make the filling, beat the cream cheese with the vanilla sugar. Spread gently in the base. Then arrange the raspberries in a pattern in the cream cheese with the holes facing down. Reserve the remaining raspberries to use as decoration and to serve as an extra with the tart.

**3** Melt the redcurrant jelly in a pan and bring to the boil. Remove from the heat and add the liqueur. Allow this to cool a little, so it will not melt the filling, and generously brush over the fruit to glaze it.

**4** Once it has set, decorate with redcurrant leaves if you wish and serve with raspberries you have not used. It is best eaten on the same day.

# APPLE AND CUSTARD TART

This tart has an apple base and is topped with a generous layer of crème pâtissière. It allows you to enjoy the subtle textures of the custard as well as the classic flavours of an apple tart.

I x **pastry ingredients** *(see page 63)*

**5 eating apples, peeled, cored and sliced**

**30g butter**

**I teaspoon cinnamon powder**

**4 egg yolks**

**60g caster sugar**

**I teaspoon vanilla essence**

**275ml** (CBN 8½) **milk**

**3 level teaspoons gelatine powder**

**4 egg whites**

**1** First make the pastry to the end of step 2 on page 63. Preheat the oven to 180°C/350°F/Gas Mark 4.

**2** Whilst the pastry is chilling, make the apple compote. Place the apples in a pan with the butter and 2 tablespoons of water over a low heat. Cook for about 15 minutes or until they break down into a mush. Stir in the cinnamon and leave to cool.

**3** Roll out the pastry and line a 24cm tart tin. Bake blind for 20 minutes (see instructions in step 5 on page 63). Remove the paper and dried beans, brush with egg wash and bake for a further 5 to 10 minutes until it is cooked and lightly browned.

**4** To make the custard filling, beat the egg yolks with the sugar and the vanilla essence. Bring the milk to the boil and pour slowly over the egg yolks, stirring all the time. Return this mixture to the pan and cook for a couple of minutes until it thickens slightly, then set aside and allow to cool to room temperature.

**5** Sponge the gelatine in a couple of tablespoons of water, then heat over simmering water until it goes liquid. Mix this into the custard well.

**6** Beat the egg whites until they form stiff peaks. Once the custard has cooled to room temperature and solidified, fold in the whites.

**7** Place the apple compote in the tart base and cover with the custard. Cover lightly with tin foil and place this in the fridge to set for at least 30 minutes. To serve, remove from the tin and blowtorch or put under a hot grill to lightly brown the top.

# APPLE FRANGIPANE TART

SERVES 8

▸ THIS RECIPE CONTAINS NUTS ◂

This is a glorious marriage of apple and almond cake, wonderfully enhanced by a sticky glaze.

- **1 x pastry ingredients** (*see page 63*)
- **100g butter**
- **100g** (CBN 3½) **caster sugar**
- **2 eggs**
- **100g** (CBN 7) **ground almonds**
- **3 eating apples, cored, peeled and halved**
  (*see Note on the opposite page*)
- **1 tablespoon flour**
- **110g apricot jam**
- **1 tablespoon Grand Marnier**

**1** Make the pastry to the end of step 4 on page 63 and then put in the fridge until needed.

**2** Cream the butter and sugar together. Beat in the eggs, almonds and flour. Pour this into the pastry case and arrange evenly.

**3** Slice each half apple crosswise and press down sideways so the half moon slices overlap. Pick this up with a palette knife and place in the tart. Repeat with the other halves, so the apple slices are arranged artistically in a circle on the base.

**4** Bake in the oven for 10 minutes, then reduce the heat to 170°C/325°F/Gas Mark 3. Bake for a further 20 minutes, or until the mixture has risen and is lightly browned.

**5** Remove from the tart tin and set to one side.

**6** Heat the jam with the liqueur so it melts and combines, then brush it over the pudding. Serve warm.

*Note:* *To prevent discolouration in peeled apples (and pears) simply brush exposed flesh with a citrus juice (lemon, lime or orange).*

# APRICOT PUFF PASTRY TARTS

Fresh apricots taste great, but when they are cooked, they take on a new dimension. This is a very rapid way to make delicious tartlets. They can be ready in 30 minutes from start to finish, and are then obviously eaten in much less time than that.

**340g pack of puff pastry**
**6 apricots, stoned and sliced**
**caster sugar, for sprinkling**

**1** Preheat your oven to 200°C/400°F/Gas Mark 6.

**2** Roll out the puff pastry so it is about 39cm by 26cm. Then cut it in half so it is 13cm by 39cm then cut each of these in 3 so you have 6 squares. Line a baking tray covered with greaseproof paper and then place the squares on it.

**3** Score a line all around the squares, 1cm in from the edge.

**4** Arrange the apricot slices within the scored line.

**5** Sprinkle the fruit with a little sugar and then bake them in the oven for about 15 minutes, or until the pastry has puffed up and has lightly browned. They are now ready to serve.

# CHOCOLATE TART

SERVES 8

Chocolate fills this tart to the very corner. It can be given subtle nuances of other flavours by adding a shot of the relevant liqueur. I do however enjoy it most in its pure form.

> I x **pastry ingredients** (see page 63)
> 215g (CBN 7) **caster sugar**
> 5 **egg yolks**
> 5 **egg whites**
> 175g **dark chocolate**
> 175g **butter**
> 60g (CBN 3) **cocoa powder**
> **pouring cream, to serve**

**1** Make the pastry to the end of step 6 on page 63 then turn the oven down to 150°C/300°F/Gas Mark 2.

**2** To make the filling, beat half of the sugar into the yolks with a spoon and in a separate bowl beat the other half into the whites in the same way.

**3** Melt the chocolate in a heatproof bowl over simmering water with the butter and the cocoa. Pour this into the yolk mixture and mix well. Add the egg whites to the mixture and mix until it is homogenised but don't whisk it and try to avoid getting air into the mixture.

**4** Pour the filling mixture into the prepared pastry case. Bake in the oven for 20 minutes or until the filling has solidified. Remove from the tin and serve warm or cold with cream.

# DOME TART

➤ THIS RECIPE CONTAINS NUTS ◄

I have named this after the Greenwich Dome because of its physical appearance. The Dome was not brown and unfortunately not chocolate but this tart has a dome of chocolate with spikes around the sides.

 1 x **pastry ingredients** *(see page 63)*
 150ml (CBN 4½) **double cream**
 100g **dark chocolate**
 125g **chestnut purée**
 **icing sugar, for dusting**

**1** Make the tart case using the recipe on page 63.

**2** Put the cream in a pan and bring to the boil, remove from the heat and mix in the chocolate until it is fully combined. Allow to cool to room temperature. Then mix in the chestnut purée and mix well.

**3** Place in the fridge for 30 minutes. Whisk the mixture until it forms stiff peaks. Put the mixture in the prepared pastry case, making it higher in the middle and use a spatula to create large even spikes with the mixture. Return to the fridge until ready to serve.

**4** Just before serving, remove from the tin and dust with a little icing sugar to give it its white tent exterior.

# FIVE-STAR JAM TARTLETS

SERVES 6

These are so good that they are in a different league from anything ready-made. Bursting to the seams with chunks of sweet fruit, they are the jam tarts fit for a king.

**1x pastry ingredients** *(see page 63)*
**410g tin of black cherries in syrup, drained, halved and stoned**
**275g cherry jam**
**clotted cream, to serve**

**1** Make the pastry to the end of step 3 on page 63.

**2** Roll the pastry out and line six individual 10cm tartlet tins. Prepare according to step 5 and bake blind for 15 minutes. Remove the paper and beans and bake until they turn a golden brown.

**3** To make the filling, add the cherries to the pan with the jam and cook over a medium heat until the jam is bubbling and it is all nice and hot.

**4** Pour this into the tartlets, allow to cool just long enough to solidify. Serve while still warm, with clotted cream.

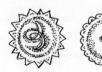

# LEMON AND LIME MERINGUE TART

SERVES 8

Forget the days of lemon meringue pie – this is something else: a tart with the combined citrus zing of lemon and lime piled high with a mountain of meringue. A truly awe-inspiring sight.

115g (CBN 6) **flour**
125g **butter**
9 **eggs**
5 **limes**
2 **lemons**
195g (CBN 7) **caster sugar**
65g (CBN 3) **cornflour**
450g (CBN 22) **icing sugar**

**1** Rub in the flour with 75g of the butter and the finely-grated zest of 1 lime, until it looks like breadcrumbs. Add ½ a tablespoon of caster sugar and mix into a dough with ½ a beaten egg. Then place in the fridge for 30 minutes to rest.

**2** In the meantime, make the filling. Separate the remaining 8 eggs and grate the zest of the lemons and limes, then juice them.

**3** Measure the juice and make it up to 570ml with water. Place in a pan and add the remaining caster sugar. Heat over a medium heat until it dissolves.

**4** Mix 60g of the cornflour with 100ml of water, mix until dissolved and then add to the juice with the egg yolks and the rest of the butter. Bring this to the boil stirring well. Cook for a couple of minutes until it thickens slightly and then leave the filling to cool.

**5** Preheat your oven to 200°C/400°F/Gas Mark 6. Roll out the pastry and line a 24cm tart tin. Bake blind in the oven for 15 minutes, remove the greaseproof paper and beans then bake for a further 5 minutes. Then remove the pastry from the oven and turn the oven down to 150°C/300°F/Gas Mark 2.

**6** Whisk the egg whites with the icing sugar and the rest of the cornflour in a bowl over some just-simmering water. Use an electric hand whisk if you have one, as this will take a while. Keep doing it until it is thick and glossy. Then take it off the heat and slowly whisk it until it cools.

**7** Place the filling in the tart case and pile up tablespoons of the meringue to reach bacchanalian heights. Bake in the slightly cooler oven for 40 minutes or until golden, then serve warm.

# LEMON TART

SERVES 8

I like to cook this one gently to get a very pure yellow tart. If you want more colour, you can sprinkle the top with granulated sugar and caramelise it.

> 1 x **pastry ingredients** (see page 63)
> **5 eggs**
> **150ml** (CBN 4½) **double cream**
> **250g** (CBN 8) **caster sugar**
> **3 lemons**
> **granulated sugar, for sprinkling (optional)**

**1** Make the pastry case to the end of step 6 on page 63, then turn the oven down to 150°C/300°F/Gas Mark 2.

**2** To make the filling, mix the eggs and double cream together. Add the sugar, the juice of 3 lemons and the zest of 2 lemons.

**3** Pour the filling mixture through a sieve into the prepared pastry case. Bake in the oven for 10 minutes or until the filling has solidified. Remove from the pastry tin and serve warm or cold.

**4** If you wish to brûlée the tart, sprinkle the top evenly with granulated sugar. Then either blowtorch it or put it under a hot grill, until the sugar melts and goes a wonderful golden brown. Remove from the heat and serve.

# ORANGE CUSTARD TART

### SERVES 8

The creamy base of this tart is deliciously contrasted with the fresh orange slices on the top. It can be served warm or cold, and is a great end to a meal.

**1 x pastry ingredients** (see page 63)
**4 oranges**
**300ml** (CBN 9) **milk**
**2 eggs**
**3 egg yolks**
**120g** (CBN 4) **caster sugar**
**40g** (CBN 2) **flour**

**1** Make the pastry to the end of step 4 on page 63 and then place in the fridge until it is ready to be filled.

**2** Preheat your oven to 180°C/350°F/Gas Mark 4.

**3** Now make the orange custard. Juice and finely grate the zest of 3 oranges. Bring the milk to the boil, add the grated rind and remove from the heat.

**4** Beat the whole eggs and extra yolks with the sugar until it is smooth and pale. Add the flour slowly to ensure there are no lumps and finish off by mixing in the orange juice. Stir in the milk and leave to cool.

**5** Pour the filling mixture into the chilled pastry case and bake in the oven for about 45 minutes, or until the custard sets.

**6** Peel and thinly slice the remaining orange. Use this to decorate the top in a pattern that identifies a good portion size and serve.

# REDCURRANT MERINGUE TART

SERVES 8

A wonder to behold. The combination of meringue and red-currants creates the effect of a lunar landscape, only in glorious technicolor. The brilliant red shows through in little circles below the lightly browned crunchy meringue.

160g butter
560g (CBN 19) caster sugar
4 egg yolks
160g (CBN 8) flour
1 teaspoon baking powder
2 egg whites
600g redcurrants, de-stalked, plus a sprig
   to decorate

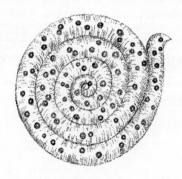

**1** Preheat your oven to 210°C/415°F/Gas Mark 6½.

**2** Beat the butter in a bowl until it is light and fluffy. Once it is creamed, beat in 160g of sugar. Then one by one add the egg yolks and mix in well. Sieve on the flour and baking powder, stirring as you go to combine it all.

**3** Cover a baking tray in greaseproof paper. Put the mixture in a piping bag. Using a thick, plain nozzle, draw a 25cm circle. Working from the outside in, make a spiral of the mixture until it is a solid circle to the centre. Bake in the oven for 10 minutes. remove and then turn the oven down to 200°C/400°F/Gas Mark 6.

**4** Whilst you are waiting for this, whisk the 2 egg whites with the remaining 400g of sugar until they form stiff peaks. Gently fold in the redcurrants.

**5** Spread the meringue on top of the base with a spatula and return to the oven.

**6** Bake for 30 to 40 minutes, until the meringue is lightly browned. Then remove from the oven and immediately cut around the edge with a knife to make a perfect circle. Serve straightaway while still hot, with a sprig of redcurrants to decorate.

# RHUBARB AND FRANGIPANE TART

SERVES 8

➤ THIS RECIPE CONTAINS NUTS ◀

This tart is quite simply amazing. The slightly acidic tang of the rhubarb is complemented exquisitely by the hint of lemon in the almond filling. The raspberry base makes it even better. If you only try one tart in this book, try this. Whilst it serves 8, I recommend having it for fewer as it really is superb cold and two really can eat a lot of it.

 I x **pastry ingredients** *(see page 63)*
 100g **butter**
 100g (CBN 3½) **caster sugar**
 **finely grated zest of I lemon**
 **2 eggs**
 100g (CBN 7) **ground almonds**
 15g (CBN 1) **flour**
 90g **raspberry jam**
 **2 medium to large sticks of rhubarb,**
   **sliced in 1cm pieces**
 40g (CBN 2½) **flaked almonds**
 60g **apricot jam**
 **I teaspoon peach schnapps**
 **custard, to serve** *(see page 145)*

**1** Make the pastry to the end of step 2 on page 63.
**2** Preheat the oven to 180°C/350°F/Gas Mark 4.

**3** Whilst the pastry is in the fridge, make the filling. Cream the butter and sugar together with the lemon zest. Beat in the two eggs one by one, making sure that each one is mixed in well before adding the next. Stir in the ground almonds and the flour.

**4** Roll out the pastry and line a 24cm tart tin.

**5** Spread the raspberry jam on the bottom of the tart, then add the filling. Press the rhubarb slices into the filling in a decorative manner. Sprinkle with the flaked almonds and leave to rest in the fridge for fifteen minutes.

**6** Bake in the preheated oven for 10 minutes, then reduce the heat to 160°C/325°F/Gas Mark 3 and cook for a further 30 minutes. It is ready when the top is a light brown and springy to the touch.

**7** Melt the apricot jam and peach schnapps together with a couple of teaspoons of water. Allow the mixture to cool a little and then brush over the tart to glaze. Serve warm with lashings of custard.

# RHUBARB AND ORANGE TART

## SERVES 8

Rhubarb's sharp taste and soft texture give plenty of scope for unusual and memorable puddings. Here it is combined with oranges, redcurrant jelly and Cointreau to give a sophisticated combination of flavours and a great climax to a meal.

I x **pastry ingredients** *(see page 63)*
**500g rhubarb, cut into chunky 4cm slices**
**2 eggs**
**165g** (CBN 5½) **caster sugar**
**50g** (CBN 2½) **flour**
**finely grated zest of I orange**
**150ml** (CBN 4½) **double cream**
**3 tablespoons redcurrant jelly**
**I tablespoon Cointreau**

**1** Sprinkle the rhubarb with 90g of the sugar and leave on one side.

**2** Make the pastry to the end of stage 6 on page 63, but only bake it blind for 10 minutes.

**3** Beat the eggs and remaining sugar together, stir in the flour, orange zest and cream.

**4** Arrange the rhubarb slices in the bottom of the tart and pour in the mixture. Bake this in the oven for 30 minutes or until the custard has set.

**5** Melt the redcurrant jelly with the Cointreau in a pan over a medium heat and then brush it over the tart.

# PASSION FRUIT TART

SERVES 8

This great tart is bursting with the unmistakeable aromas and flavour of the fine passion fruit. The brûlée top makes it distinctive and colourful.

**I x pastry ingredients** *(see page 63)*
**4 eggs**
**160g** (CBN 5½) **caster sugar**
**160ml** (CBN 5) **double cream**
**150ml** (CBN 4½) **passion fruit juice (about 10 fruits)**
**granulated sugar, for sprinkling**

**1** Make the pastry to the end of step 4 on page 63 but preheat the oven to 180°C/350°F/Gas Mark 4.

**2** Beat the eggs and caster sugar together, then mix in the cream and juice. Strain this through a sieve into the chilled pastry and bake in the oven for 30 to 40 minutes.

**3** When the tart has set, remove it from the oven. Sprinkle the top with granulated sugar and brûlée under a hot grill or with a blowtorch. Serve warm with any remaining passion fruits.

# SPICY PEAR AND GINGER TART

SERVES 6

This tart is a bit like a cake in texture, but it has a superb caramelised, fruity bottom and exquisite spicy flavours. The ginger brings out the best in the pears and the cinnamon makes the whole thing smell and taste delicious.

110g butter
200g (CBN 7½) **soft brown sugar**
5 pears
185g (CBN 9) **flour**
270g (CBN 9) **caster sugar**
2 teaspoons cinnamon powder
1½ teaspoons baking powder
1 teaspoon salt
2 eggs
150ml (CBN 4½) **sunflower oil**
1 teaspoon grated fresh ginger
2 tablespoons vanilla sugar *(see Note page 7)*
300ml (CBN 10) **cream**

**1** Preheat the oven to 180°C/350°F/Gas Mark 4. Mix together the butter and brown sugar, put in a 20cm cake tin and place in the preheated oven.

**2** Peel, core and slice 4 of the pears into 6 segments. Arrange these in a circular pattern in the now molten butter and sugar mixture.

**3** Peel, core and grate the other pear. Mix well with all the remaining ingredients, sieving in the flour and mixing well to avoid lumps. Mix until a light brown paste is formed.

**4** Place this mixture on top of the pears in the cake tin and bake in the oven for 1 hour.

**5** To serve, turn out onto a warm plate.

**6** To make the vanilla cream, mix vanilla sugar with whipped cream. Serve this with the warm tart.

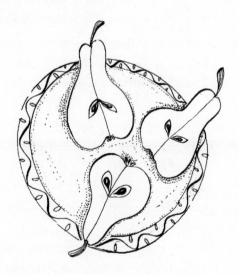

# STRIPY JAM TART

SERVES 6

This is a simple but tasty tart. The slits in the pastry on the top create a wonderful stripy effect.

**340g pack of puff pastry**
**250g of your favourite jam**
**I egg**
**I dessertspoon milk**
**granulated sugar, for sprinkling**

**1** Roll the pastry into two rectangles, one measuring 20cm by 45cm and the other 15cm by 40cm. Prick the larger rectangle all over with a fork and spread the jam evenly over the pastry, leaving a clean border 2½cm from the edge.

**2** Take the second piece of pastry and gently fold it in half so it is 12½cm by 40cm. Cut lines through the pastry from side to side, starting at the folded over edge and stopping 1cm before the 'open' edge. These should be cut at 1cm intervals. When you open the pastry again, you should have slits in the centre, but a solid border all the way round.

**3** Wet the clean border edges of the jam-filled rectangle with a little water. Then unfold the pastry with the slits so it covers the top. Press the edges together and leave in the fridge for 20 minutes to rest. Preheat your oven to 230°C/450°F/Gas Mark 8.

**4** Beat the egg and milk together to make an egg wash. Paint this on the surface of the tart and sprinkle with a little granulated sugar. Bake in the oven for 20 minutes and then turn down the heat to 200°C/400°F/Gas Mark 6. Bake for another 30 or 40 minutes. If it is browning too much, cover it lightly with some tin foil. It is ready when the sides are firm and crispy. I prefer to eat this hot, but it is equally good cold.

# WHITE CHOCOLATE AND ORANGE MERINGUE TART

SERVES 8

The tart is piled high with a wonderful orange-scented meringue top, which hides a sensual white chocolate filling. A surprise for first-timers, but an eagerly anticipated treat for those in the know.

**75g butter, diced**
**175g** (CBN 9) **flour**
**25g dark chocolate**
**200g** (CBN 6½) **caster sugar**
**4 eggs, separated**
**50g cornflour**
**I teaspoon vanilla essence**
**65ml** (CBN 2) **milk**
**200g white chocolate**
**zest of I small orange**
**orange cream, to serve** (see Note below)

**1** To make the pastry base, rub the butter into the flour until it resembles breadcrumbs. Then grate in the dark chocolate, add 25g of sugar and mix together. Add an egg yolk and a couple of teaspoons of water, and mix until it forms a dough. Wrap in clingfilm or tin foil and put in the fridge for 30 minutes to rest.

**2** Once it has rested, preheat your oven to 200°C/ 400°F/Gas Mark 6.

**3** Roll out the pastry using a little flour to prevent it from sticking. Line a 24cm tart tin with the pastry and follow the instructions in steps 5 and 6 on page 63.

**4** To make the filling, mix the cornflour with 3 yolks, the vanilla essence and a little of the milk. Mix well until a smooth paste forms. Use a whisk to beat out any remaining lumps. Heat the milk and add the paste to the hot milk, stirring well all the time. Cook it for a couple of minutes over a low heat. Then grate in the white chocolate, stirring until it melts in. Pour this thick custard mixture into the tart shell.

**5** To make the meringue, whisk 4 egg whites adding the sugar bit by bit as you go. When the whites form stiff peaks, add the orange zest and mix in.

**6** Spread the meringue on top of the tart and put it under a hot grill for a few minutes until the top browns. This can now be served hot or cold. I prefer to serve it hot with a little orange cream.

*Note:* *To make orange cream, simply finely grate the zest of a small orange into 150ml of double cream. Add a tablespoon of caster sugar and whip to firm peaks.*

# APRICOT, LEMON AND ALMOND TART

## SERVES 8

▸ THIS RECIPE CONTAINS NUTS ◂

This is a lovely tart, which combines the flavours of apricots with a dash of citrus zest and almonds. The lemon prevents any risk of over richness from the almonds.

**I x pastry ingredients** *(see page 63)*
**300g butter**
**300g** (CBN 10) **caster sugar**
**300g** (CBN 22) **ground almonds**
**finely grated zest and juice, I lemon**
**3 eggs**
**450g apricots, halved and stoned**
**whipped cream, to serve**

**1** Make the pastry to the end of step 2 on page 63.

**2** Preheat the oven to 180°C/350°F/Gas Mark 4. Roll out the pastry and line a 24cm tart tin. Bake this blind (see instructions for preparation in step 5 on page 63) for 15 minutes, then remove the greaseproof paper and dried beans and bake for another 5 minutes.

**3** Cream the butter and sugar together and stir in the almonds. Mix in the zest and juice of the lemon. Beat the eggs in one by one, allowing each one to be fully combined before you add the next.

**4** Pour into the pastry and push the apricots flat-side down into the mixture. Bake in the oven for about 40 minutes or until it has risen and is lightly browned.

**5** Serve with a little whipped cream whilst still warm.

# TARTE TATIN

SERVES 8

This is a simple version of the traditional French favourite in which delectable caramel apples are enveloped in pastry.

   **1 x pastry ingredients** *(see page 63)*
   **50g butter**
   **150g** (CBN 5) **caster sugar**
   **6 eating apples, peeled, quartered and cored**
   *(see Note on page 69)*

**1** Make the pastry to the end of step 2 on page 63.

**2** Preheat your oven to 200°C/400°F/Gas Mark 6. Melt the butter and add to a 24cm one-piece tin, with the sugar. Mix together. Arrange the apples on the bottom, touching the butter and sugar as much as possible.

**3** Roll out the pastry so you have a 30cm circle. Put this over the top of the apples and tuck down around the sides. Pierce the top in a few places with a skewer.

**4** Place this over a medium heat on a stove for a few minutes to get the sugar caramelising. Bake it in the oven for 30 minutes. When it is ready, free the edges by running a knife around them gently and turn out upside down onto a plate. You will have the wonderful caramelised apples on top.

# UPSIDE-DOWN SUMMER FRUIT TART

SERVES 6

▸ THIS RECIPE CONTAINS NUTS ◂

This is a great way to combine a selection of summer fruits. The tart is cooked and then turned over like a Tarte Tatin; only when it is turned, it is much more colourful.

butter, to grease
500g summer fruits, e.g. raspberries, strawberries, redcurrants
2 eggs
50g (CBN 1½) caster sugar
1 tablespoon flour
50g (CBN 3½) ground almonds
vanilla ice cream, to serve

**1** Preheat the oven to 180°C/350°F/Gas Mark 4.

**2** Butter the bottom of a 24cm tart tin and cut out a piece of greaseproof paper to fit the bottom. Make sure it is not a two-piece tin or it will make a bit of a mess.

**3** Place the fruit evenly around the bottom of the tin.

**4** Whisk the eggs and sugar together for a few minutes until the mixture is quite fluffy and holds a shape when you swirl it.

**5** Fold in the flour and almonds and pour over the fruit. Bake in the oven for 15 minutes, or until the top sets. Turn this out onto a plate and serve warm with vanilla ice cream.

FIRE
& ICE

Fire and Ice are both of vital importance in cooking. The recipes in this section either have flames or are frozen, both in the case of Raspberry Baked Alaska. A well-placed sheet of flames can do wonders to a pudding. It looks fabulous and adds depth to the flavours. As gadgets go, one of my favourites is my blowtorch, which has a plethora of uses in the kitchen.

Like so many people, I love ice creams for their fantastic tastes and special cool textures. Ice creams and sorbets thrive on the variety of fruits and ingredients available nowadays. So use the basic recipes given here and go forward using your favourite ingredients. The only limit is your own imagination.

# TIPS ON
# ICE CREAM AND
# SORBET MAKING

An ice cream machine is a great piece of equipment. It allows you quickly to make wonderful puddings. Serving homemade ice cream made from scratch is a very impressive 'pudding in a panic'. You do not, however, need to have a machine to make ice cream and I have included some recipes which do not need one. The technique is quite simple: you freeze the ice cream or sorbet solid, then break it up and liquidise it. You then stiffly whip two egg whites and fold them into the mixture. You can now refreeze this and serve when wanted. Ice cream and sorbets made this way do not always have the same texture, but there is no harm in this. I have also included my 'cheat' method, where you just freeze it and it comes out ready.

# AMARETTO ICE CREAM

SERVES 6

➤ THIS RECIPE CONTAINS RAW EGG ◀

With its rich almond flavour, Amaretto tastes like liquid marzipan. It produces a very full-flavoured ice cream that accompanies other puddings well.

> **850ml finest vanilla ice cream**
> **2 tablespoons amaretto**
> **finely grated zest of 1 orange**
> **½ teaspoon vanilla essence**

**1** Cut the ice cream into small pieces and beat with a spoon until it is light enough to mix in the additional ingredients.

**2** Mix in the amaretto, orange zest and vanilla essence.

**3** Place in an airtight container then return to the freezer and chill until it solidifies, then serve.

# CHOCOLATE MUD ICE CREAM

SERVES 8

This is a real chocolate experience, enhanced by the choco-late-coated raisins that are a lovely surprise. Beware of this over-the-top ice cream, it's very rich.

**6 egg yolks**
**140g** (CBN 4½) **caster sugar**
**4 tablespoons cocoa powder**
**275ml** (CBN 8½) **milk**
**400g dark chocolate, chopped into small pieces**
**570ml** (CBN 18) **double cream**
**170g chocolate-coated raisins**

**1** Beat the egg yolks and sugar together.

**2** Place the cocoa in a pan with the milk and bring to the boil. Remove from the heat and melt half of the chocolate into it.

**3** Whilst this is still hot, pour it over the egg mixture and whisk all the time. Return to the pan and cook over a low heat until it thickens, then allow to cool.

**4** Once it is cool, lightly whip the cream. Add the cream, raisins and the rest of the chocolate. Freeze in an ice cream machine.

# BANANA FLAMBÉ

SERVES 6

This is a great chance to show off a bit. The flames are large and the spices attract the attention of every nose in the area.

6 bananas
grated zest and juice of 1 lemon
50g butter
40g (CBN 1½) soft brown sugar
1 teaspoon cinnamon powder
½ teaspoon ground nutmeg
grated zest and juice of 1 orange
3 tablespoons Grand Marnier
vanilla ice cream, to serve

**1** Peel the bananas and slice them in half lengthways.

**2** Cover the bananas with the lemon juice to prevent them browning.

**3** Put the butter and sugar in a frying pan with the spices. Cook over a medium heat until the butter melts and they are all mixed together nicely.

**4** Add the bananas to the pan with any leftover lemon juice.

**5** Add the orange zest and juice to the pan with the lemon zest and mix into the liquid. Allow the bananas to cook until they brown lightly, turning as necessary.

**6** Heat the Grand Marnier in a separate pan, ignite with a flame and pour over the bananas. Cook until the flames have died down and serve with vanilla ice cream.

# BEER SORBET

This is a novel pudding, but it is very refreshing and brings out the full flavours of a traditional ale. It is ideal for a sunny afternoon.

> **25g** (CBN 1) **caster sugar**
> **1 tablespoon white wine vinegar**
> **570ml** (CBN 18) **real ale**

**1** Place the sugar in a pan with 1 litre of water. Bring it to the boil and simmer until it becomes a syrup that falls off the spoon in a thin thread. Remove from the heat and allow it cool.

**2** Mix in the vinegar and a quarter of the beer. Put the mixture in an ice cream machine and freeze it.

**3** To serve, place a scoop in a tall glass and top up with beer. Stir until it froths, sit back and enjoy.

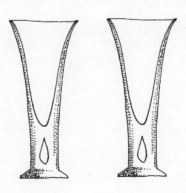

# BLACKCURRANT LEAF SORBET

## SERVES 6

This is an amazing sorbet. It does not have the colour of the blackcurrants, but manages to have the flavour. Its opaque shades really do disguise its natural inner strength. Serve as a palate cleanser between courses or as an accompaniment to a rich pudding. I use leaves picked from the garden, as they are not readily available from supermarkets.

**225g** (CBN 7½) **caster sugar**
**2 large handfuls of blackcurrant leaves,**
   **washed and drained**
**juice of 3 lemons**

**1** Place the sugar in a pan with a 570ml of water. Bring it to the boil and simmer for a couple of minutes.

**2** Dunk the blackcurrant leaves in the hot syrup. Mix them around and allow their flavours to seep into the syrup as it cools.

**3** Sieve to take out the leaves. Add the lemon juice to the mixture.

**4** Allow to cool and then freeze in an ice cream machine.

# CHAMPAGNE SORBET

## SERVES 6

This is the peak of epicurean overindulgence. It is surprisingly easy to make, but simply devastating. Use this to wow the pickiest of people or to lure the loveliest.

**225g** (CBN 7½) **caster sugar**
**1 bottle of champagne or sparkling wine**
**frosted grapes, to serve** (see Note below)

**1** Place the sugar in a pan with 275ml of water. Bring it to the boil slowly, stirring to allow it to dissolve. Once boiled, simmer for a few minutes and set aside to cool.

**2** Once it is cool, add the champagne and freeze in an ice cream machine.

**3** To serve, use a melon baller to put small balls into a bowl champagne glass. Decorate with frosted grapes and serve.

*Note: There are two ways of making frosted grapes. You can either lightly coat them in egg white and roll them in granulated sugar. Or, if you are worried about eating raw egg, you can make a syrup out of equal amounts of sugar and water. Bring this to the thread stage (where a thread of the sugar is brittle) and roll the grapes in it and allow them to cool.*

# FLAMBÉED FRUIT KEBABS

This is a rather fun way of cooking fruit. It can be done outside on a barbecue, or if the weather gets the better of you, you can use a grill. These have quite a high alcohol content, but that is why they burn so well. The fruits here are some of my favourites, but you can use whatever you want to. Use seasonal, tasty fruits that you like. Complement them by using an appropriate liqueur, e.g. crème de framboise, with red fruits.

> **4 peaches**
> **4 apricots**
> **20 cherries**
> **200ml** (CBN 6½) **peach liqueur**
> **120g** (CBN 4) **caster sugar**

**1** Cut the peaches and apricots in half and remove all stones and stalks.

**2** Put all the fruit in a bowl and cover with the liqueur. Leave to macerate for about 20 minutes. Strain the fruit, reserve the liquid in a small pan and thread the fruit onto 4 skewers.

**3** Put them on the skewers in any order you prefer to make a pretty pattern, for instance: cherry, apricot, cherry, peach, cherry, apricot, cherry, peach, cherry.

**4**  Sprinkle the sugar all over the kebabs. The fruit will be sticky from the liqueur, so the sugar will stick well.

**5**  Put the kebabs on a clean barbecue or under a hot grill. Leave them for about 6 to 7 minutes or until they have caramelised, turning as necessary.

**6**  Put the kebabs on a heatproof plate. Heat up the remaining liquid and light with a match. Pour all over the kebabs and serve with a flourish.

# FROZEN CHOCOLATE SOUFFLÉ

SERVES 6

➤ THIS RECIPE CONTAINS RAW EGG ◄

For those of you who have trouble making soufflés, look no further. This frozen chocolate soufflé is made to look as if it has risen to extreme heights, and will not collapse on you on the way to the table.

**90g dark chocolate**
**3 eggs**
**50g** (CBN 1½) **caster sugar**
**350ml** (CBN 10½) **double cream**
**cocoa powder**

**1** Wrap tin foil around the edge of 6 ramekin dishes to make a collar that extends a couple of inches above the top.

**2** Melt the chocolate by placing it in a heatproof bowl over simmering water and stirring it until melted.

**3** Separate the eggs and beat the yolks with the sugar in a heatproof bowl. Place this over a pan of simmering water and whisk until it thickens slightly and the sugar has dissolved. Do not overcook or you will have sweet scrambled eggs.

**4** Mix the chocolate into this and mix well. Keep whisking the mix until it cools to room temperature.

**5** Whip the cream and egg whites in separate bowls until they each form stiff peaks. Fold in the cream, then the egg whites. Divide this mixture up between the ramekins and place in the freezer for a couple of hours to freeze.

**6** To serve, remove the collars gently and dust with a little cocoa.

# FROZEN LEMON YOGHURT

## SERVES 6

You can add any flavour to frozen yoghurt, but I love the tart taste of lemon in this recipe. It is very refreshing and invigorates a tired palate with its clean, crisp taste.

**100g** (CBN 3½) **caster sugar**
**finely grated zest and juice of 3 lemons**
**1150ml** (CBN 34) **natural Greek style yoghurt**

**1** Place the sugar in a pan with 150ml of water over a medium heat. Stir well to allow the sugar to dissolve and bring to the boil, then remove and allow to cool.

**2** Mix the lemon zest and juice into the yoghurt, and mix in the cooled syrup.

**3** Freeze in an ice cream machine; depending how big it is, you may have to do this in two goes.

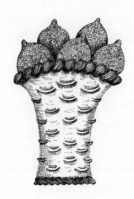

# FROZEN ORANGE PIE

SERVES 6

➤ THIS RECIPE CONTAINS RAW EGG ◄

This is an old recipe, handed down on a stained and crumpled piece of green notepaper, and is one of my favourite puddings. The concentrated flavour of the oranges rests on a fabulous biscuit base and is cloaked with a layer of cream.

> 12 digestive biscuits
> 25g (CBN 1) soft brown sugar
> 1 teaspoon cinnamon powder
> 75g butter
> 2 eggs
> 75g (CBN 2½) caster sugar
> 2 oranges
> 1 lemon
> 300ml (CBN 9) cream
> 2 teaspoons vanilla sugar (see Note on page 7)

1 Preheat your oven to 180°C/350°F/Gas Mark 4.

2 This pudding has a biscuit base, so the first thing to do is make it. Break the digestive biscuits up by putting them in a clean plastic bag and hitting them gently with a rolling pin until they turn into crumbs.

3 Place the crumbs in a bowl and mix in the brown sugar and cinnamon.

4 Melt the butter and stir it into the biscuit base. Press this mix into a 24cm tart tin so that it covers the base and sides. Bake in the oven for 6 minutes.

5 To make the filling, separate the eggs and mix the yolks with 25g of the caster sugar. Grate in the zest of 1

orange and half the lemon, then squeeze in the juice of the oranges and lemon.

**6** Mix together well in a saucepan over a low heat. Stir well until it thickens. Then remove and allow to cool.

**7** Beat the egg whites and remaining caster sugar until they form stiff peaks. Fold this into the orange custard. Whip 150ml of the cream until it forms soft peaks and fold this in as well.

**8** Pour this mixture into the biscuit base and freeze for at least 2 hours. Half an hour before serving, whip the remaining 150ml of cream with the vanilla sugar and spread it over the pie. Return it to the freezer for 20 minutes and then serve.

# FRUIT YOGHURT BRÛLÉE

## SERVES 6

This is a great way to use up leftover bits of fruit and I like to use seasonal soft fruit. But it is also so much more than a great way to use up ingredients. Think of the voluptuous yoghurt enveloping the fruit, topped with the sizzling caramel – now that's more like it!

> **230g fruit of your choice, chopped into bite sized pieces**
> **340g** (CBN 10) **plain yoghurt**
> **¼ teaspoon nutmeg**
> **250g** (CBN 8½) **caster sugar**
> **1 tablespoon vanilla sugar** *(see Note on page 7)*

**1** Mix most of the fruit into the yoghurt with the nutmeg and vanilla sugar, reserving a small amount of fruit to decorate.

**2** Place this concoction in 6 ramekins and top with the remaining fruit. Make sure that there is 1cm of space before the top of the ramekin for the caramel.

**3** Put the sugar in a pan with 275ml of water. Bring to the boil and simmer until forms a beautiful golden brown caramel. Pour this onto the tops of the puddings. It will set quickly and then you can serve.

# GINGER ICE CREAM

SERVES 6

➤ THIS RECIPE CONTAINS RAW EGG ◀

Ginger is a wonderful ingredient that is equally at home with both sweet and sour tastes. It makes an excellent accompaniment and brings a hint of spice to any dish. This recipe does not require an ice cream machine.

> **6 eggs**
> **150g** (CBN 5) **caster sugar**
> **450ml** (CBN 14) **double cream**
> **1 teaspoon vanilla essence**
> **90g stem ginger candied in syrup, diced**

**1** Separate the eggs and whisk the whites with the sugar until they form stiff peaks.

**2** Whip the cream with the vanilla essence until it forms firm peaks. Whip the egg yolks separately and then fold them into the cream. Fold this into the egg whites and freeze for 30 minutes.

**3** Fold the ginger into the ice cream and freeze until needed.

# GOOSEBERRY AND ELDERFLOWER SORBET

### SERVES 4

Gooseberry and elderflower bushes could not be more different if they tried. There is however a certain magic when their flavours marry together. They form a refreshing and light sorbet that is excellent as a palate cleanser or pudding.

100g (CBN 3½) **caster sugar**
**3 elderflower heads, checked for bugs**
**225g gooseberries**
**white seedless grapes, to serve**

**1** Put the sugar in a pan with 570ml of water. Bring to the boil slowly, stirring continuously to ensure all the sugar dissolves. Simmer for 5 minutes, put the elderflower heads in a heatproof bowl and then pour the syrup over them. Leave to infuse for 30 minutes.

**2** Stew the gooseberries in a little water over a medium to low heat. When they collapse and are cooked, liquidise them and pass the mixture through a sieve. Strain the elderflower syrup and combine with the gooseberry mixture.

**3** Freeze in an ice cream machine and serve with cold, white seedless grapes.

# GRAPE SORBET

SERVES 4

This is a very elegant sorbet for the over-indulgent. It can be served as an exquisite palate cleanser, or as an accompaniment to a pudding of character.

**1kg white grapes.**
**400g** (CBN 13½) **caster sugar**
**frosted grapes, to serve** *(see Note on page101)*

**1** Roughly chop the grapes and push them through a fine sieve; this should give you about a 570ml of juice.

**2** Put the sugar in a pan with 275ml of water. Bring to the boil slowly, stirring well to make sure the sugar dissolves. Simmer for a few minutes until the liquid becomes a light syrup in texture. Remove from the heat and allow to cool.

**3** Put the syrup and grape juice together and freeze in an ice cream machine or as explained on page 95 if you don't have a machine.

**4** Use a melon baller to make small balls of the sorbet. Refreeze them so they are hard. Serve in a bowl champagne glass with a few frosted grapes. If you have time, you can use lots of balls on a plate to form a full sized bunch of grapes with the whole sorbet.

# ICED CHOCOLATE ORANGES

SERVES 6

➤ THIS RECIPE CONTAINS RAW EGG ◄

These combine great flavour with great presentation. The two-tone effect of the orange and brown is a stunning colour contrast, set off so well by the textured orange of the shell.

**7 oranges**
**55g** (CBN 2) **caster sugar**
**2 egg yolks**
**570ml** (CBN 18) **double cream**
**45g dark chocolate**

**1** Cut the tops off 6 of the oranges and scoop out the flesh. Put the flesh in a bowl and freeze the shells and tops. If you place the shells in a bun tray they are easier to deal with later.

**2** Put the sugar in a pan with 150ml of water and bring it to the boil. Simmer for a couple of minutes to make a syrup. Put the yolks in a bowl and pour the syrup over them slowly, whisking all the time until they cool.

**3** Finely grate the zest of the remaining orange and mix with half of the cream. Whisk the cream until it forms soft peaks and fold in half of the yolk and syrup mixture. Half-fill the orange shells with this and freeze.

**4** Melt the chocolate in a bowl over a pan of simmering water. Once it has melted, mix in the rest of the cream and allow to cool. Then whip this so it forms soft peaks and fold in the rest of the yolk and syrup mixture. Fill up the oranges with this and put on their tops.

**5** Freeze for at least 3 hours. To serve, allow them to soften a little and very carefully cut them in quarters lengthways with a very sharp knife. If you are worried about this, serve them whole. They will still look and taste great.

# MELON SORBET SURPRISE

## SERVES 6

Here you are assaulted by a riot of colour that is bursting to get out. The vivid red of the raspberry sorbet is set off by the subtle shades of green in the melon. The flavours are even better than the colour and the marriage of the melon and raspberry is excellent, heightened by the contrast of chilled melon and sensual raspberry. This is a true feast for both the eyes and taste buds.

150g (CBN 5) **caster sugar**
**500g raspberries**
**juice of 1 lemon**
**2 ripe galia melons**

**1** To make the syrup, put the sugar and 150ml of water in a saucepan. Bring to the boil, stirring until all the sugar has dissolved. Simmer for 5 minutes and allow to cool.

**2** Pick out the best raspberries for decoration and set aside. Then liquidise the raspberries and strain to remove the pips.

**3** Strain the lemon juice into the raspberry purée, with the cooled syrup.

**4** Place the mixture in an ice cream machine to freeze. If you do not have one, follow the instructions at the beginning of the chapter (see page 95).

**5** Chop the melons in half and remove the seeds with a spoon. Then put in the freezer for a good 20 minutes. Fill the hollows with the sorbet and smooth over, then return to the freezer for another 20 minutes. To serve, slice the melon and serve with the reserved raspberries.

# PINK GRAPEFRUIT SORBET

I use pink grapefruit as it has a magnificent deep colour and lots of flavour; I feel that this is reflected well in the sorbet. You can make this with white grapefruit, but to my mind it reduces its allure.

**110g** (CBN 6½) **caster sugar**
**5 pink grapefruits**

**1** To make the syrup, put the sugar in a pan with 150ml of water. Bring it to the boil slowly, stirring to make sure it all dissolves. Simmer for a couple of minutes and allow to cool.

**2** Squeeze the grapefruits into a bowl – there should be about a 570ml of juice.

**3** Add the syrup to the juice – it should taste a bit too sweet. Then freeze it in an ice cream machine.

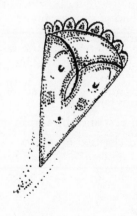

# RASPBERRY BAKED ALASKA

SERVES 8

This is for the more outlandish cook who feels showmanship is all part of the fun. This has flames, a riot of colour, and tastes magnificent. No more the boring vanilla ice cream centre in soggy sponge – surely this is the only way forward.

1250ml **raspberry sorbet**
3 **eggs**
460g (CBN 15½) **castor sugar**
**finely grated zest of 1 lemon**
1½ **teaspoons vanilla essence**
60g (CBN 3) **flour**
50g **clarified butter** (see Note on page 27)
10 **egg whites**
4 **tablespoons vodka**

**1** Place the sorbet on a board and bash it around until it forms a cylinder about 30cm long, then return it to the freezer.

**2** Make the genoise sponge, preheat the oven to 180°C 350°F/Gas Mark 4.

**3** Butter and line a 32.5 by 23cm swiss roll tin with greaseproof paper. Beat 3 eggs with 110g of the sugar until the mixture falls from the whisk in thick ribbons. Add the lemon zest and the vanilla essence. Gently fold in the flour and clarified butter.

**4** Place the mixture in the tin and bake in the oven for about 30 minutes or until the top is spongy and it is starting to come away from the sides in places. Allow to cool a little, and whilst still warm, wrap it around the ice cream and return to the freezer until needed.

**5** Preheat the oven to 230°C/450°F/Gas Mark 8. To make the meringue whisk the egg whites with the rest of the sugar until they form stiff peaks. Take the sorbet and sponge from the freezer and place on a large heat-proof dish or oven tray. Cover it with the meringue and raise the meringue with a knife to form spikes. Bake in the oven for a few minutes until the meringue has browned on top.

**6** Heat and ignite the vodka, pour it all over the pudding and serve flaming.

# ICE CREAM CHEAT

➤ THIS RECIPE CONTAINS RAW EGG ◄

This is my 'cheat' ice cream. It is a basic recipe and can be used to make almost any flavour. It makes quite a light, fluffy ice cream, which is delicious and needs no ice cream machine. The best thing is that you can make it any flavour you want, so have fun experimenting.

**750g fruit**
**275ml** (CBN 8½) **double cream**
**4 egg whites**
**6 tablespoons caster sugar, plus extra to sweeten**

**1** Remove any stones, pips or inedible skin from the fruit. Place in a food processor and liquidise to make a fruit coulis.

**2** Beat the cream to soft peaks in a bowl and fold in the fruit coulis. If you are using tart fruit, add some sugar to it until it is sweet.

**3** Whisk the egg whites with the sugar until they form stiff peaks. Then fold them into the rest.

**4** Place this in an airtight container and freeze until needed.

# SORBET CHEAT

This is my basic sorbet recipe and you can use it to make almost any flavour you desire. So let your imagination run wild – use whatever you can think of. As long as it tastes good before you freeze it, it should taste great once it is a sorbet.

**200g** (CBN 6½) **sugar**
**600ml fruit purée**
**lemon juice, to taste (optional)**

**1** To make the syrup, put the sugar in a pan with 570ml of water. Bring to the boil slowly, stirring well to allow it to dissolve. Simmer for a few minutes until it forms a light syrup and then leave to cool.

**2** Mix the fruit purée with the cooled syrup. Taste it – it should taste a bit too sweet, as it will lose sweetness when frozen. If necessary, add more sugar and if too sweet, add some lemon juice, to taste.

**3** Freeze in an ice cream machine. Store in an airtight container in the freezer until needed.

# A LITTLE BIT
# EXTRA

This section is a combination of two things: extras to go with puddings and little nibbles to have after or instead of them. It is sometimes hard to think of something different and original to serve with a pudding, so here are a few ideas, as well as the essential homemade custard. There are however times when you want to pull out all the stops and the meal does not stop at the pudding. I am of course talking about those lovely little extras you want on special occasions with the coffee. So instead of the traditional after dinner mint, why not really indulge your guests and make some yourself. They can be quite time consuming, but are worth every second.

# PURE CHOCOLATE TRUFFLES

Chocolate truffles come in a variety of flavours, but this is the original. The clean taste is enhanced by the sharp dryness of the cocoa dusting. This is one for the purist.

**125ml** (CBN 4) **double cream**
**500g dark chocolate**
**100g** (CBN 5) **cocoa powder, for dusting**

**1** Place the cream in a saucepan over a low heat. Break in half the chocolate stirring until it melts. When fully combined, remove from the heat and allow to cool to room temperature.

**2** Line a 32.5cm x 23cm swiss roll tin with clingfilm and fill with the mixture. Then chill for 2 hours in the fridge.

**3** Chop the filling into 2cm squares. On a board dusted with cocoa, roll them into balls.

**4** Melt the rest of the chocolate in a heatproof bowl over hot water. Using two forks, dip the truffles in the chocolate, allowing them to rest until semi-set and then roll in the cocoa. Leave them to set fully and then lightly knock off any excess cocoa. Keep in a cool place until ready.

# APPLE TURNOVERS

MAKES 16

Apple turnovers are an old favourite – they are also quick to make, especially if you already have the filling ready. You can, of course, substitute a cherry compote or something similar for the apple filling. These little delicacies are excellent for almost every occasion.

**5 dessert apples, cored, peeled and sliced**
**2 tablespoons caster sugar**
**I teaspoon cinnamon powder**
**340g pack of puff pastry**
**I egg**
**I dessertspoon milk**
**granulated sugar, to sprinkle**
**custard, to serve**

**1** Put the apple slices in a pan with a 4 tablespoons of water and cook over a medium heat, stirring occasionally until they start to dissolve. Add the sugar and cinnamon and cook until the purée is quite thick, then remove from the heat.

**2** Preheat the oven to 190°C/375°F/Gas Mark 5.

**3** Roll out the pastry quite thinly and cut out 16 circles, each about 7–8cm across. Divide the apple mixture into 16 portions and place a portion on one half of a circle. Fold the circles in half and seal the edges together.

**4** Mix the egg with the milk and brush the pastries with this egg wash. Score decorative lines across the top of the pastry with a sharp knife and sprinkle with a little granulated sugar.

**5** Bake in the oven for 10 to 15 minutes, or until the pastry puffs up and browns lightly on top.

# CHOCOLATE BISCUITS

MAKES ABOUT 25

▸ THIS RECIPE CONTAINS NUTS ◂

These thin biscuits are quick to make and can be on the table before you know it. They are excellent accompaniments to creamy puddings and make a purchased pudding look much more interesting.

140g butter

140g (CBN 4½) **caster sugar**

2 eggs

100g (CBN 5) **flour**

2 tablespoons cocoa powder

50g (CBN 3½) **flaked almonds**

1 teaspoon cinnamon powder

**1** Preheat your oven to 200°C/400°F/Gas Mark 6.

**2** Cream the butter with 125g of sugar until light and fluffy. Then beat in the eggs one at a time.

**3** Mix together the flour and cocoa and sieve into the butter and egg mixture. Stir well and spread the mixture onto greaseproof paper so that it is about 5mm thick.

**4** Mix together the remaining 15g of sugar, cinnamon, and flaked almonds. Sprinkle evenly across the biscuit. Then place it in the oven for about 20 minutes. When the almonds have browned it is ready.

**5** Remove from the oven and, using a knife or pastry cutters, cut the biscuits into shapes on the tray. Do this quickly before it cools and hardens. The biscuits taste best if eaten on the same day.

# CHOCOLATE ORANGE MARSHMALLOW FUDGE

This is a wonderfully smooth and sticky concoction. The marshmallow gives it a stunningly original texture which is springy but in no way rubbery. The flavours are superb together and it is very addictive. It melts in your mouth and is an indescribable fusion of the different ingredients. It is sensational after dinner but just as good when nibbled in the middle of the day. Can you have just one piece?

**juice and finely grated zest of 1 large orange**
**100g marshmallows**
**90g butter**
**175g dark chocolate**
**200g milk chocolate**
**½ teaspoon vanilla essence**

**1** Put the marshmallows, orange juice and butter in a pan. Cook over a low heat until the marshmallows melt.

**2** Remove from the heat and add the rest of the ingredients. Stir until it has all melted into a nice smooth mixture.

**3** Line a loaf tin with clingfilm and fill with the fudge. Allow the fudge to set. Once it has set, cut it into slices and serve.

**4** You can experiment by serving it in different shapes. Try cutting it into thin rectangular strips, or use pastry cutters to give interesting shapes.

# CHOCOLATE BROWNIES

## MAKES 20 PIECES

> THIS RECIPE CONTAINS NUTS (OPTIONAL) ◄

Chocolate brownies are a great thing. These ones are especially gooey. I have left out the traditional walnuts because I don't like them. If you do, just chop 50g of them and stir in before baking.

100g (CBN 3½) **caster sugar**
225g (CBN 8) **soft brown sugar**
25g (CBN 1) **cocoa powder**
100g **butter, plus extra for greasing**
2 **egg yolks**
175g (CBN 9) **flour**
¼ **teaspoon bicarbonate of soda**
50g **walnuts (optional)**

**1** Place the sugar in a saucepan with 150ml of water. Stir over a medium heat until the sugar dissolves, then bring to the boil. Simmer until it reaches the fine thread stage (see Note on page 5)

**2** Turn off the heat and stir in the cocoa powder. Stir well with a whisk until it has dissolved fully into the syrup and there are no lumps.

**3** Preheat your oven to 180°C/350°F/Gas Mark 4.

**4** Butter a 23cm square tray and line with greaseproof paper.

**5** Beat the butter in a bowl until it is smooth and creamy. Beat in the yolks one by one until they are fully absorbed into the mixture.

**6** Stir in the chocolate syrup until it is well mixed in. Then sieve in the flour and bicarbonate of soda and fold gently into the mixture (fold in walnuts now if using).

**7** Pour into the tin and bake in the oven for about 40 minutes until cooked.

**8** When cooked, allow the tin to cool. Whilst still warm, cut the brownies into squares and remove from the tin.

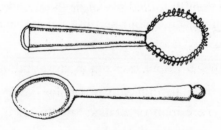

# CITRUS BISCUITS

MAKES ABOUT 30

These biscuits are wonderfully tasty and very quick to make. So I make them a lot when I go skiing. You can make up the dough before you go out and leave it in the fridge. When you get back, all you need to do is shape and cook them. In minutes, you are greeted by the wonderful smells wafting out from the oven. Then, it is no time at all before they are cooled and on the table as a little something to help you keep up your strength after a hard day on the slopes.

> **220g butter**
> **110g** (CBN 3½) **caster sugar**
> **275g** (CBN 14) **self-raising flour**
> **1 orange or 2 lemons**

**1** Preheat your oven to 180°C/350°F/Gas Mark 4.

**2** Cream the butter with the sugar. To do this, beat the butter and sugar together with a wooden spoon until it goes a light creamy colour and has a fluffy texture. You can also do this in a food processor.

**3** Next, sieve the flour over the mixture and mix well.

**4** Choose the flavour you want for your biscuits. Whether it is lemon or orange, simply grate the zest finely and combine with the biscuit dough.

**5** Make small balls out of the dough. Line a baking tray with greaseproof paper. Place the dough balls on the tray, leaving a good gap between each one and press them down to make them into a biscuit shape.

**6** Bake in the oven for about 10 minutes or until they are cooked and lightly browned. Serve and devour.

# FLORENTINES

➤ THIS RECIPE CONTAINS NUTS ◀

These are a superb fusion of chocolate and sticky biscuit which makes an oh-so-special sticky nibble. Make lots, as they tend to disappear when your back is turned.

- 115g butter, plus extra for greasing
- 115g (CBN 4) caster sugar
- 2 tablespoons golden syrup
- 115g (CBN 6) plain flour
- 1 teaspoon ground ginger
- 45g mixed peel, chopped finely
- 150g glacé cherries, chopped finely
- 45g (CBN 3) flaked almonds
- 200g chocolate of your choice

**1** Preheat your oven to 180°C/350°F/Gas Mark 4.

**2** Combine the butter, sugar and syrup in a saucepan over a low heat. Remove from the heat and mix in the flour and ginger.

**3** Add the cherries, the mixed peel and the almonds and mix well.

**4** Butter a baking tray. Place teaspoons of the mixture on the tray and push each down into a circle. Leave spaces between them, as they will spread. Bake in the oven for about 5 to 10 minutes. They are cooked when they have spread and browned. Take them out, remove them with a spatula to a wire rack and allow to cool.

**5** Melt the chocolate and drizzle over the biscuits. I like to use both white and dark chocolate.

# LEMON MACAROONS

MAKES ABOUT 25

▸ THIS RECIPE CONTAINS NUTS ◂

This is a great twist on a traditional favourite. The lemon gives it more colour and certainly more flavour. They are served in pairs glued together by a sweet lemon butter. Use them to give texture to a gooseberry fool or any other liquid pudding.

**2 eggs**
**120g** (CBN4) **caster sugar**
**3 lemons**
**150g butter**
**250g** (CBN 18) **ground almonds**
**250g** (CBN 12½) **icing sugar**
**6 egg whites**

**1** To make the custard mix the 2 eggs with the caster sugar, the zest of 2 lemons and the juice of half a lemon. Once well mixed, place this in a heatproof bowl over simmering water and stir until it thickens. Pass through a sieve to remove any lumps and cool.

**2** Beat the butter until it is softened, whisk in the custard for a few minutes until it is very well combined and pales. Then refrigerate.

**3** Preheat your oven to 180°C/350°F/Gas Mark 4. Mix the ground almonds and icing sugar in a bowl with the zest of the last lemon.

**4** Whip the egg whites until they form stiff peaks and fold in the almond and sugar mixture. Pipe this mixture in 5cm circles onto greaseproof paper or rice paper, if you have it. Place them in the oven for about 10 minutes until cooked. Remove from the oven and allow to cool on a wire rack.

**5** Ensure the filling is at room temperature or you will crush the biscuits. Once the macaroons have cooled, place a teaspoon of the filling on the bottom of one and press down with the bottom of another so that they are joined. Keep them in an airtight box until needed.

# PEACH DREAMS

These little beauties are made to look like peaches, but the fun does not stop there. The combination of the white chocolate and peach truffle filling with the white chocolate covering is the stuff dreams are made of. These make the perfect gift or hedonistic indulgence.

**60ml** (CBN 2) **double cream**
**600g white chocolate**
**4 tablespoons peach schnapps or liqueur**
**icing sugar, as needed**
**red food colouring, to decorate**

**1** Place the cream in a bowl over some simmering water. Break in 250g of the chocolate. Stir until it all dissolves.

**2** Add the schnapps or liqueur and mix in well. Place in the fridge to chill for 2 hours, then beat until it makes soft peaks.

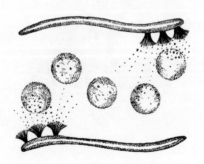

**3** Line a 32.5cm x 23cm swiss roll tin with clingfilm and fill with the mixture. Chill in the fridge for 6 hours to set thoroughly.

**4** Chop the mixture into 2cm squares and roll them into balls using a little icing sugar.

**5** Melt the rest of the white chocolate in a bowl over simmering water. With two forks, dip the truffles in the chocolate and then leave them to set on greaseproof paper.

**6** For this final step, I recommend covering the surrounding area, as this can be a messy process. Put a little red dye on the end of a toothbrush and flick it gently over the white chocolate truffles to create a speckled effect. Then present to the lucky recipients.

# RASPBERRY SWEETIES

MAKES ABOUT 35

I love the taste of raspberry and feel that it is the ideal partner for chocolate. It can be made sharp so it cuts through a sickly pudding or soft so it oozes sweetness and flavour. This is a superb recipe for some little bonbons.

125ml (CBN 3½) **double cream**
50g **raspberry jam**
250g **dark chocolate**
25g **butter, diced**
25ml (CBN 1) **raspberry schnapps or liqueur**
350g **milk chocolate**
**a few perfect raspberries, to decorate**

**1** Place the cream in a saucepan with the jam over a low heat. Break the dark chocolate into pieces and stir it in. When it has melted, remove it from the heat. Add the butter to the mix with the schnapps or liqueur. Mix well until the butter has melted and is completely homogenised with the rest of the mixture. Then leave the mixture in the fridge for 1 hour to set.

**2** Line a 32.5cm x 23cm swiss roll tin with clingfilm and place the set mixture in it. Spread it around so it is 1½ cm deep. Return to the fridge for 6 hours, until it is well chilled.

**3** Cut your sheet of filling into pieces 1½ cm wide by 3cm long.

**4** Melt the milk chocolate in a bowl over some simmering water. Using two forks, dip pieces of filling in the milk chocolate and leave to set on baking parchment. To create a pattern of lines across the width of the chocolate, use the prongs of a fork to touch the chocolate on the top.

**5** Serve on an elegant platter with a few carefully arranged perfect raspberries.

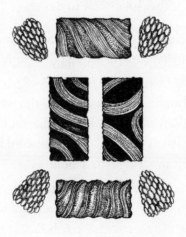

# ROCKY ROAD

This really is the rocky road to ruin. It is full of all those wonderful things that are fattening. It is so good, it should be banned, and then smuggled around the world so as to ensure a good supply.

> 300g milk chocolate
> 100g marshmallows, chopped,
>   or mini marshmallows
> 4 digestive biscuits, broken into nibble sized pieces
> 200g glacé cherries, quartered
> 50g mixed peel
> sunflower oil, for greasing

**1** Melt the chocolate in a bowl over simmering water. Once it has melted, mix in the rest of the ingredients and stir until they are all coated in chocolate.

**2** Lightly oil some tin foil and spread the whole mixture thickly on it. Roll into a thick sausage and carve generous slices once it has cooled, or allow it to cool and cut into triangles.

# STICKYFIED GOO-GOOS

## MAKES ABOUT 25

These sticky, chewy things are a danger to dentures. They do have the redeeming feature of tasting marvellous and are one of the first things I ever cooked. They may turn out pink, but they are ambrosial.

   **110g butter**
   **1 pack of plain toffees, unwrapped**
   **1 pack of marshmallows**
   **50g Rice Krispies**

**1** Melt the butter in a pan over a medium heat. Add the toffees and marshmallows. Stir occasionally until they have melted.

**2** Remove from the heat and gently fold in the Rice Krispies.

**3** Place dessertspoons-full of the mixture in paper cases. Repeat until you have used up all of the mixture and set aside to cool.

**4** Once they have cooled, get chewing.

# SURPRISE SHORTBREADS

### MAKES ABOUT 20

I love the idea of surprises. These are orange shortbread biscuits with a very simple chocolate and cream cheese filling. But they are made much more exciting because you are not expecting the chocolate centre.

125g butter
60g (CBN 3) icing sugar
finely grated zest of 1 orange
125g (CBN 6) self-raising flour
60g cornflour
60g dark chocolate
60g cream cheese
1 egg yolk
1 dessertspoon milk
granulated sugar, to sprinkle

**1** Cream the butter and sugar together until light and fluffy. Then mix in the orange zest and stir in the flour, cornflour and a tablespoon of water. Beat this mixture until it is completely smooth and even. Cover and refrigerate to allow it to rest.

**2** While this is resting, you can make the filling. Melt the chocolate in a bowl over some simmering water. Beat the cream cheese until it is soft and malleable and stir in the molten chocolate.

**3** Preheat your oven to 180°C/350°F/Gas Mark 4. After at least 30 minutes, remove the dough and roll it out to about ½ cm thick. Cut into 5cm round biscuits – a champagne flute is the perfect size for this if you don't have pastry cutters.

**4** Take half the biscuits and put ½ teaspoon of the chocolate mixture on each. Beat the egg with the milk. Brush this egg wash around the edge of the biscuits with the mixture on. Then put a plain biscuit on top and stick down. Repeat this until all the biscuits are made. Brush their tops with the egg wash and sprinkle with granulated sugar. Line a baking tray with greaseproof paper. Arrange the biscuits on leaving at least 3 or 4cm between each one.

**5** Bake the biscuits in the oven for 10 to 15 minutes or until golden. Allow to cool on a wire rack and serve.

# SWEET 'MUSHROOMS'

MAKES 25

These are both sweet to look at and to taste. They create a miniature field of 'mushrooms' just waiting for some giant to devour them. They are actually made of meringue but look incredibly like mushrooms. They are great for children's parties or even as after-dinner petit-fours.

**225g** (CBN 7½) **caster sugar**
**4 egg whites**
**cocoa powder, for dusting**
**175g dark chocolate**

**1** Beat the sugar and egg whites well until they form good, stiff peaks.

**2** Set the oven to 110°C/225°F/Gas Mark ½ .

**3** Cover two baking sheets with greaseproof paper and wipe with a piece of kitchen roll with a little tasteless cooking oil on it.

**4** Put the meringue in a piping bag with a round nozzle about 1cm across. On one sheet, make 25 circles about 4cm across and about 1cm high. These are going to be the caps of the mushroom, so make the tops domed and smooth. On the other sheet, make 25 vertical towers about 3½ cm high. To do this, you will need to make the bottom a bit thicker and cut it off when you get to the right height with a knife.

**5** Lightly dust the tops of the 'domes' on the first baking tray with a little cocoa. Then put both trays in the oven for 3 hours.

**6** Melt the chocolate in a heatproof bowl over simmering water and spread a little on the underside of the domes. Put them 'dome sides' down in a bun tray so they don't wobble and place the stalks on top of the chocolate-covered side. When they have set, they are ready to present and serve. They should even stand up on their own.

# MADELEINES

These are wonderful little French cakes. The only problem is as they are such a good snack size it is hard to have just one. Hand them round with ice cream or have them as a full-blown pudding, by stuffing them with fresh fruit and whipped cream. They are also sinful when dipped in chocolate fondue.

>150g butter, plus extra for greasing
>150g (CBN 4½) caster sugar
>2 eggs
>160g (CBN 8) plain flour
>zest of I lemon
>½ teaspoon baking powder

**1** Preheat the oven to 220°C/425°F/Gas Mark 7.

**2** Beat the butter with the sugar until it turns pale and fluffy. Beat in the eggs one by one, making sure each egg is fully mixed in before adding the next.

**3** Mix the flour with the lemon zest and the baking powder. Mix this into the butter and sugar mixture.

**4** Butter a madeleine tray (this is the one with scallop-like indents). If you do not have one, use a small muffin tray in the same way. Fill these up three-quarters of the way with the mixture and bake in the oven for about 10 minutes.

**5** Once they have risen and are lightly browned around the edges, remove from the oven and allow to cool on a wire rack.

144          A LITTLE BIT EXTRA

# PROPER CUSTARD

MAKES ABOUT 500ML

Some puddings really need proper custard, not just for the sake of tradition but for the whole taste sensation. It is easy to make and you really can't beat it.

> **75g** (CBN 2½) **caster sugar**
> **4 egg yolks**
> **425ml** (CBN 13) **milk**
> **I teaspoon vanilla essence**

**1** Beat the sugar and egg yolks together in a bowl until they lighten in colour and go a little fluffy.

**2** Bring the milk to just under the boil and gently pour into the bowl with the egg yolks, beating all the time.

**3** Mix in the vanilla essence and return it to the pan. Cook over a low heat, stirring well until it thickens but do not let it boil. The custard is now ready.

# INDEX

---